EMBROIDERED
BAGS & PURSES

©2004 Country Bumpkin

First published in North America by

krause publications
An F+W Publications Company

700 East State Street • Iola, WI 54990-0001
715-445-2214 • 888-457-2873
www.krause.com

Our toll-free number to place an order or obtain
a free catalog is (800) 258-0929

ISBN 0-9750920-2-2

EDITOR
Heather Moody

EDITORIAL ASSISTANTS
Anna Scott, Marian Carpenter

GRAPHIC DESIGNERS
Lynton Grandison, Jenny James

PATTERN DESIGNERS
Sarah Kent, Jennie Victorsen

ILLUSTRATIONS
Kathy Barac

PHOTOGRAPHY
Andrew Dunbar

PUBLISHER
Margie Bauer

Printed in China

Bags, purses, pouches, sachets, totes... You will find them all in this collection. Bags for every occasion and every mood. Bags simply stitched or elaborately embroidered and embellished. Bags which can be created by all stitchers from the beginner to the expert.

Bags are not only an essential accessory, they can also be an expression of the wearer's personality or mood. Embroidery, in its many manifestations, is the perfect medium to reflect this. From the subdued colours and restrained stitching of *Bird of Paradise* to the ebullient colours and texture of the *Elizabethan Sweetbag* and the romantic pastels of *Celadon*, there can be no doubt about the message the bag conveys to the rest of the world.

Because of their function - to house anything from just the bare essentials to half one's worldly possessions, or perhaps to cope with a serious shopping expedition - the bag takes on many forms. We have introduced some tiny bags to hold small treasures, a dainty cosmetic purse which makes a perfect gift, and a voluptuous lavender sachet to scent your lingerie.

Then there are the more business-like - but nevertheless pretty - bags which can cope with a day out and about, such as *All Roses* and *Country Life*.

The evening bag presents an opportunity to display a little frivolity and extravagance. Beads can be lavished on silk purses such as *Blue Danube* to reflect the excitement of a special occasion.

By creating your own bag to suit an outfit, occasion or mood you can show off your genius and express your individuality. The materials are easily sourced and need not be expensive, while the skills are quickly learnt. With time - which you have to find - and inspiration - which we have provided - you can be the owner of a stunning wardrobe of bags and purses!

Stumpwork, beading, casalguidi, smocking and conventional surface embroidery are explained, as well as construction methods for a variety of styles.

The detailed instructions, step-by-step photographs and stitch glossary will guide you in creating the perfect bag.

Bag n. flexible container with an opening at one end.

Purse n. 1. small bag or pouch, often made of soft leather, for carrying money esp. coins. 2. U.S. a woman's handbag.

Pouch n. a small flexible baglike container

Sachet n. a small soft bag containing perfumed powder, placed in drawers to scent clothing.

Tote bag n. a large roomy handbag or shopping bag.

CONTENTS

ELIZABETHAN
SWEETBAG

by Susan O'Connor

The reign of
Elizabeth I heralded
a stellar period for
floral embroidery.

Elizabeth was a very keen embroiderer and in many of her portraits, her clothing displays the rich embroidered embellishment that was typical of the period.

Gifts of embroidery were very popular amongst nobility and the sweet bag was one of the most common gifts. Not intended for everyday use, the bag would often contain money, perfume or sweetmeats and was richly decorated with embroidery in silk and metal thread. As personal hygiene at this time was almost non-existent (bathing was considered hazardous to the health), carrying a sweet smelling bag when going out was almost a necessity. These bags were usually purchased from professional embroiderers at great cost. The motifs used depicted popular flowers and insects and often employed raised stitches to give an extra dimension to the stitching. Metal threads added to the high cost of these bags as they were made from gold and silver.

The design for this bag is based on the elegant scrolling vines that are commonly seen in embroidery from this period. The vines form a framework for the flowers that are created using bullion knots and needlewoven picots. Although the bullion knot was not in common use at this time, its raised appearance makes it perfect for this style of embroidery.

Needle weaving and detached blanket stitch were often used to create raised motifs that could be lifted away from the surface of the fabric, sometimes revealing further embroidery underneath.

Soft gold silk damask is used for the front of our bag and the back is heavy silk satin. The strawberry pink lining is silk dupion and all the threads used are silk. A small amount of gold thread is used to whip the border stitches and create the bee wings. All the flowers depicted - roses, English daisies, heartsease, daffodils and forget-me-nots, were popular during the 1600s.

Susan O'Connor has based her design for this utterly gorgeous sweetbag on the rich colours and textures that were favoured in Elizabethan times.

REQUIREMENTS

Fabric

21cm x 19cm wide (8 1/4" x 7 1/2") piece of gold silk damask

19cm x 16cm wide (7 1/2" x 6 1/4") piece of gold silk satin

16cm x 38cm wide (6 1/4" x 15") piece of strawberry silk dupion

Supplies

90cm (36") gold rayon cord

20 vintage silver sequins

Invisible thread

15cm (6") embroidery hoop

Long quilting pins

Tracing paper

Sharp HB pencil

Threads & Needles

See page 12.

PREPARATION FOR EMBROIDERY

See the liftout sheet for the embroidery design and pattern.

Transferring the design

Using a fine black pen, trace the embroidery design onto tracing paper. Tape the tracing to a window or light box. Place the damask fabric over the tracing, aligning the placement marks on the design with the straight grain of the fabric. Tape in place. The light shining through will make the design visible through the fabric. Using the pencil, trace the design onto the fabric.

EMBROIDERY

See page 13 for step-by-step instructions for constructing the bag.

See pages 14-17 for step-by-step instructions to work the leaf, daffodil, heartsease and English daisy.

The no. 10 milliner's needle is used for the bullion knots on the bee and the no. 3 milliner's needle for all other bullion knots.

Use the no. 28 tapestry needle for the needlewoven picots and raised cup stitch and the crewel needle for all remaining embroidery.

Order of work

Scrolling vine

Using the darker shade of green, embroider the vine in chain stitch. Using the remaining shade of green, work another row of chain stitch alongside the first. Whip the darker rows with the metallic thread. Work the detached chain leaves on the vines at the marked positions.

Daffodils

Stitch six three-thread needlewoven picots for the petals of the two full daffodils.

Work the trumpets in raised cup stitch in the centre of each flower.

Embroider three needlewoven picots for the petals of the side view daffodil. Stitch the side view cup with two rows of blanket stitch, one on top of the other.

Work the leaves, working two-thread needlewoven picots, twisting and anchoring them at the marked positions.

Work the stems in chain stitch and the receptacle in straight stitch *(diag 1)*. Anchor the petals of the full daffodil at the tip, arching them slightly.

Diag 1

Heartsease

For the full heartsease, stitch two five-thread needlewoven picots for the back petals. Work the three front petals in the same manner, stitching the centre petal last. Embroider the highlights on the front petals with the metallic thread and on the back petals with the burgundy brown silk thread. Stitch a French knot centre.

Embroider the bud with three needlewoven picots, in a similar manner to the full heartsease. Stitch a detached chain calyx over the bud. Work the stem and vein in chain and stem stitch and the leaves in blanket stitch.

THIS DESIGN USES

Blanket stitch · Bullion knot
Bullion loop · Bullion knot
Detached chain combination
Chain stitch · Coral stitch
Detached chain · Fly stitch
French knot · Needlewoven picots
Raised cup stitch · Satin stitch
Stem stitch · Straight stitch
Whipped chain stitch

English daisies

Full flower

Embroider the full daisy with bullion knot petals. Stitch a bullion knot at each of the quarter points of the middle circle (*diag 2*). Fill each quarter with four or five bullion knots (*diag 3*).

Diag 2

Diag 3

Stitch a bullion knot-detached chain combination around each of the bullion knots. Work a fly stitch around the tip of each petal. Fill the centre of each daisy with French knots.

Half flower

Work the petals for the half daisy in the same manner as the full daisy. Embroider the calyx in blanket stitch and the stem in chain stitch.

Bud

Embroider the petals for the coloured bud, working a single fly stitch around the tip of the bud, then the blanket stitch calyx. Work the green bud in a similar manner, omitting the bullion knot-detached chain combination. Work the stems in chain stitch.

Roses

Large roses

Stitch the two large roses first, working a bullion loop and two bullion knots for the centre. Embroider six inner petals and ten outer petals.

Smaller roses

Work the centres of the smaller roses in the same manner as the large roses, surrounded by six to seven petals. Stitch the leaves in bullion knots.

Large buds

Stitch a ten wrap bullion knot for the centre of the bud with a five wrap bullion knot on either side of the centre. Work a twelve wrap bullion knot on either side of the five wrap bullion knots, anchoring the end of each one at the tip of the central bullion knot (*diag 4*).

Diag 4

Stitch the calyx with four bullion knots. Work a long anchoring stitch at the tip of each bullion knot.

Small bud

Stitch an eight wrap bullion knot for the centre of the bud with a five wrap bullion knot on either side of the centre. Work a ten wrap bullion knot on either side of the five wrap knots, anchoring the end of each one at the tip of the central bullion knot. Work a French knot at the base of each bud. Embroider the stems in chain stitch.

Forget-me-nots

Beginning with chain stitch, work the stems, changing to stem stitch at the marked positions. Embroider a French knot for the centre of each flower. Stitch the five petals, working a French knot for each petal. Work French knots along the end of each stem for the buds and a fly stitch around each centre. Embroider the small leaves with five straight stitches for each leaf.

Bee

Embroider the bee with alternating bands of gold and black bullion knots. Work several horizontal stitches for the head. Surround the body with a fly stitch and work the legs and antennae with fly stitches. Work a French knot for each eye (*diag 5*). Using the metallic thread, embroider the wings with detached chains.

Diag 5

Border

Work the outer row of the border in chain stitch, whipped with the metallic thread. Work a row of coral stitch inside the previous row.

Sequins

Stitch sequins randomly around the outside of the design.

CONSTRUCTION

See page 104 for the cutting layouts and instructions for making the tassels and twisted cord.

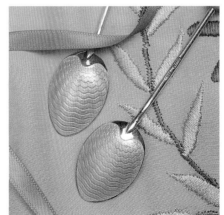

THREADS & NEEDLES

Au Ver à Soie, Soie d'Alger stranded silk

A = crème

B = 1345 royal purple

C = 2124 grass green

D = 2135 dk olive green

E = 2525 lt gold

F = 2535 dk gold

G = 4622 lt strawberry

H = 4623 strawberry

I = 4624 dk strawberry

J = 4912 cornflower

Au Ver à Soie, 100/3 silk thread

K = 625 burgundy brown

Au Ver à Soie, Bourdon

L = 6012 gold

No. 8 crewel needle

No. 3 milliner's needle

No. 10 milliner's needle

No. 28 tapestry needle

EMBROIDERY KEY

All embroidery is worked with two strands unless otherwise specified.

Scrolling vine

Vine = C and D (4 strands chain stitch), L (whipping)

Leaves = C (detached chain)

Daffodils

Full flower

Petals = E (needle-woven picot, 6 petals)

Centre = F (raised cup stitch)

Side view flower

Petals = E (needle-woven picot, 3 petals)

Centre = F (blanket stitch)

Receptacle = D (straight stitch)

Leaves = C or D (needlewoven picot)

Stems = D (chain stitch)

Heartsease

Full flower

Back petals = E (needle-woven picot, 2 petals)

Highlights = K (straight stitch)

Front petals = B (needlewoven picot, 3 petals)

Highlights = L (straight stitch)

Centre = C (French knot, 2 wraps)

Bud

Petals = B (needlewoven picot, 2 petals), E (needle-woven picot, 1 petal)

Stem = D (chain stitch)

Calyx = D (detached chain)

Leaves = C (blanket stitch, stem stitch)

Stem = C (stem stitch)

English daisy

Full flower

Petals = A (bullion knot, 10 wraps) G (bullion knot-detached chain combination, 4 wraps), I (fly stitch)

Centre = E (French knot)

Half flower

Petals = A (bullion knot, 10 wraps) G (bullion knot-detached chain combination, 4 wraps), I (fly stitch)

Receptacle = D (blanket stitch)

Stem = D (chain stitch blanket stitch)

Bud

Petals = A (bullion knot 10 wraps; 2 bullion knots 5 wraps; 2 bullion knots 12 wraps), G (bullion knot-detached chain combination, 4 wraps) I (fly stitch)

Receptacle = D (blanket stitch)

Stem = D (chain stitch)

Green bud = C (bullion knot 10 wraps; 2 bullion knots 5 wraps; 2 bullion knots 12 wraps; fly stitch)

Stem = C (chain stitch)

Roses

Large roses

Centre = I (3 strands bullion loop, 10 wraps 2 bullion knots, 10 wraps)

Inner petals = H (3 strands 6 bullion knots, 12 wraps)

Outer petals = G (3 strands 10 bullion knots, 12 - 14 wraps)

Stem = D (chain stitch)

Small roses

Centre = I (3 strands bullion loop, 10 wraps 2 bullion knots, 10 wraps)

Petals = H (3 strands 6 - 7 bullion knots, 12 wraps)

Leaves = D (2 bullion knots 5 - 7 wraps)

Stem = D (chain stitch)

Large buds

Petals = I (bullion knot 10 wraps; 2 bullion knots 5 wraps; 2 bullion knots, 12 wraps)

Calyx = D (3 strands, 4 bullion knots, 12 - 16 wraps; French knot)

Small bud

Petals = I (3 strands bullion knot, 8 wraps)

Calyx = D (3 strands, 2 bullion knots, 5 wraps; 2 bullion knots 10 wraps; French knot)

Stem = D (chain stitch)

Forget-me-nots

Stems = C (chain stitch, stem stitch)

Centres = E (3 strands French knot), A (1 strand, fly stitch)

Petals = J (3 strands, French knot)

Buds = J (3 strands, French knot)

Bee

Body = E (1 strand 3 bullion knots)

K (1 strand 3 bullion knots, fly stitch)

Head = K (1 strand, satin stitch)

Legs and antennae = K (1 strand, fly stitch)

Eyes = K (French knot)

Wings = L (detached chain)

Border = F (3 strands, chain stitch)

L (1 strand, whipping)

H (3 strands, coral stitch)

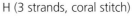

CONSTRUCTING THE BAG

The beautiful embroidery of the bag is complemented by strawberry silk lining, coral stitch edging and blanket stitch tassel loops. All seam allowances are 1cm (3/8").

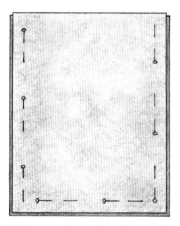

1. Trim the damask to the cutting line. With right sides together, pin the front to the back.

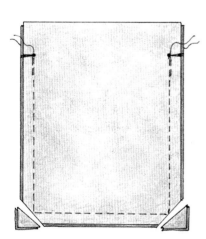

2. Beginning and ending 2.5cm (1") down from the top edge, stitch around three sides of the bag as shown above. Clip and trim.

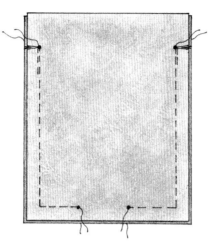

3. Cut the silk dupion in half. Stitch as for the damask, leaving an 8cm (3") opening in the base. Press the seams open. Turn to the right side.

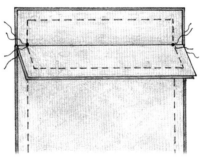

4. With right sides together, slide the bag up over the lining and stitch around each side of the top section.

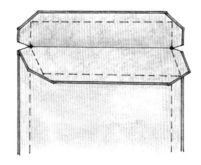

5. Trim and clip the corners.

6. Turn to the right side, through the opening in the lining. Hand stitch the opening closed and push the lining down into the bag. Press the seams.

7. Using three strands of H, work coral stitch around the edges of the bag, working 2cm (3/4") blanket stitch loops at the base at the marked positions.

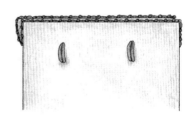

8. Stitch four 1.5cm (5/8") needlewoven bars with two strands of C, at the marked positions for the drawstring.

NEEDLE WOVEN PICOT LEAF

The picot is a lace-making technique used in stumpwork to create raised embroidery.

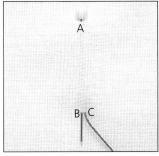

1. Foundation threads. Insert a quilters pin into fabric from A to B for 3cm (1 ¼"). This is the picot length. Bring thread to front at C and pull through.

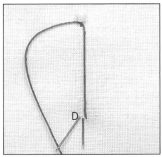

2. Wrap the thread in an anti-clockwise direction under the head of the pin. Insert the needle at D.

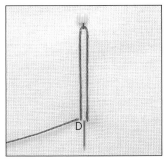

3. Pull the thread through. Re-emerge just to the left of D. Pull the thread through. Rotate the fabric 90 degrees anti-clockwise.

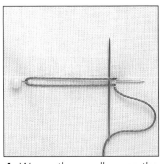

4. Weave the needle over the lower thread and under the upper thread. Do not pierce the fabric.

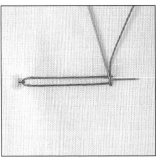

5. Pull the thread through firmly and push the wrap down onto the fabric with the tip of the needle.

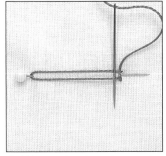

6. Weave the thread over the upper thread and under the lower thread. Do not pierce the fabric.

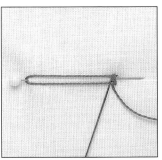

7. Pull through firmly and push the wraps down the loop with the tip of the needle so it sits snugly against the first wrap.

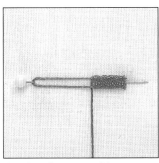

8. Continue working steps 4 - 7, weaving stitches over and under the threads of the loop. Push each wrap firmly against the previous one.

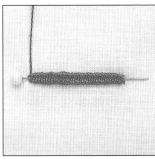

9. Continue weaving until the loop is completely filled and the wraps are firmly packed.

10. Remove the pin. Twist the picot and take the needle to the back at the desired position

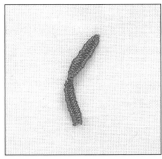

11. Pull the thread through and secure on the back of the fabric. **Completed needle woven picot leaf.**

NEEDLE WOVEN OPEN BASE PICOT

Work 6 picots for the daffodil petals.

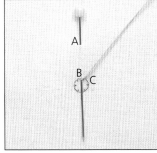

1. Mark six even spaces around the circle. Insert a pin from A to B for approx. 12mm (½"). Bring needle to front at C and pull through.

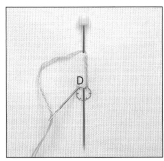

2. Wrap the thread under the head of the pin in an anti-clockwise direction. Insert the needle at D.

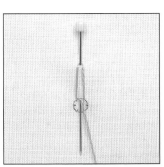

3. Pull the thread through and re-emerge just to the right of B. Pull the thread through.

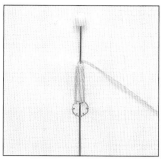

4. Wrap the thread clockwise around the head of the pin.

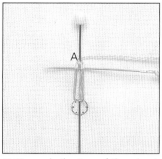

5. Towards the top of the pin at A, weave the needle from right to left over the centre thread (under, over, under).

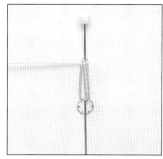

6. Pull the thread through and pull firmly up against the pin.

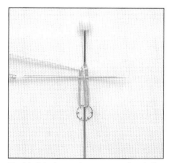

7. Hold thread taut to the left, weave the needle from left to right (over, under, over).

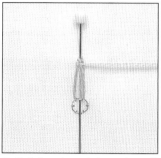

8. Pull the thread through until the loop is snug against the first thread.

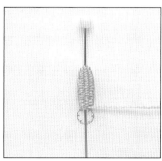

9. Continue weaving in this manner, pushing towards the tip of the picot to pack the threads tightly.

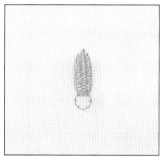

10. Take the needle to the back at the base and remove the pin. **Completed needlewoven open base picot.**

11. Work a further five petals. **Completed petals.**

12. Trumpet. Bring the needle to the front at A and take to the back at B.

13. Bring the needle to the front at C and take to the back at B. Bring the needle to the front at A and take to the back at C.

14. Bring the needle to the front inside the triangle, near C. Slide the needle under the base thread (C - A) and wrap thread anti-clockwise around needle.

15. Pull the thread through to form a knot. Work 2 - 3 knots into each of the base threads. **Completed first round.**

16. Slide the needle under the thread between the first and second stitch of the first round. Wrap the thread anti-clockwise around the needle.

17. Pull the thread through. Work each knot of the second round using the linking thread.

18. Continue until the trumpet is the desired height. Weave the needle down the side of the cup and secure on the back.

19. Anchor the petals at the tips, arching them slightly. **Completed daffodil.**

HEARTSEASE

The petals of the heartsease flower on the *Elizabethan Sweetbag* have been created using a five thread picot for each petal. Ensure that the base of the petal is not as wide as the main section.

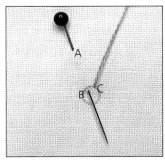

1. Back petals. Insert a long pin from A to B for approx 1cm (3/8"). This is the picot length. Bring thread to front at C and pull through.

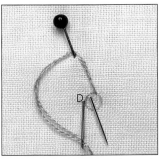

2. Wrap the thread anti-clockwise under the head of the pin. Insert the needle at D.

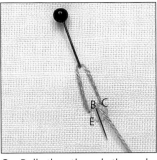

3. Pull the thread through. Bring the thread to the front between C and B at E.

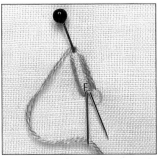

4. Wrap the thread anti-clockwise under the head of the pin. Insert the needle at F.

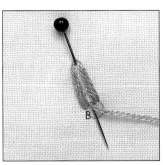

5. Pull the thread through. Re-emerge at B. Pull the thread through.

6. Wrap the thread clockwise around the head of the pin. The centre thread crosses the pin and becomes the fifth foundation thread.

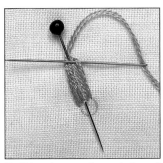

7. Take the needle and thread under the first thread and begin weaving.

8. Continue weaving, packing the threads firmly, until all the foundation threads are filled.

9. Take the thread to the back at the base of the picot (close to C) and secure. Remove the pin.

10. Catch the tip with a tiny stitch each side of the tip to give a more rounded look. **Completed petal.**

11. Work the second back petal in the same manner, slightly overlapping at the base.

12. Front petals. Work two side front petals in the same manner.

13. Work the centre front petal in the same manner, overlapping the side petals.

14. Work the highlights in straight stitch, then the French knot centre. **Completed heartsease.**

DAISY

The intriguing bullion knot - detached chain combination stitch is used to form the daisy and buds. Work a ring of bullion knots around the centre.

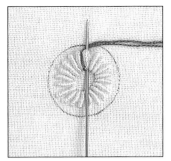

1. Bring the thread to the front at A. Take the needle to the back at B and re-emerge at C.

2. Take the thread from left to right under the tip of the needle.

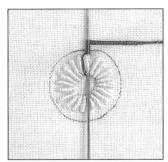

3. Wrap the thread clockwise around the needle four times.

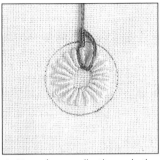

4. Ease the needle through the wraps and pull the thread through.

5. Pull the thread firmly until a tight bullion is formed at the end of the chain stitch.

6. Take needle to back. Repeat for remaining bullions. Work a fly stitch around each petal. **Completed bullion knot-detached chain combination.**

7. Fill the centre with French knots. Secure at the back. **Completed dasiy.**

WHIPPED CHAIN STITCH

Whipped chain stitch is a combination stitch. A line of chain stitch forms the foundation row. Each chain stitch is then whipped with a new thread. The whipping thread does not go through the fabric except at the beginning and end. For added interest, contrasting thread may be used for the whipping. Work the stitches downwards.

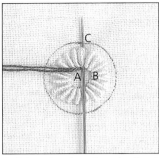

1. Foundation row. Mark your design line onto the fabric. Work a row of chain stitch following the line.

2. Whipping. Using a second thread, bring the needle to the front at A, just to the left and half-way along the first chain stitch.

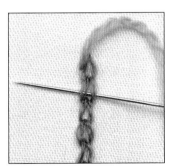

3. Pull the thread through. Take the needle from right to left under the second stitch. It does not go through the fabric.

4. Pull the thread through. **First whipped stitch.**

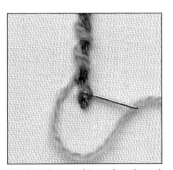

5. Continue taking the thread from right to left under each stitch. To end off, take the needle to the back under the last chain stitch.

6. Completed whipped chain stitch.

COUNTRY LIFE

As elegant as the tulip,

As romantic as a day in Spring,

As comforting as Nan's apple pie,

As sweet as the greenest apple,

As versatile as you.

by Kris Richards

Add a romantic touch to this linen bag with finely stitched embroidery. Worked in dusky hues, the garland depicts a circlet of twisting ribbon decorated with roses and clematis. A single rose surrounded by rosebuds finishes the back of the bag.

THIS DESIGN USES

Bullion knot · Detached chain
Fly stitch · French knot · Granitos
Rosette stitch · Stem stitch

REQUIREMENTS

Fabric

90cm x 112cm wide (35 1/2" x 44") beige linen/cotton blend

40cm x 112cm wide (15 3/4" x 44") beige polyester lining

Supplies

70cm x 112cm wide (27 1/2" x 44") light weight woven fusible interfacing

8cm x 21cm wide (3 1/8" x 8 1/4") piece of medium weight buckram

1.7m (1yd 31") size 1 piping cord

Empty ball point pen

Transfer paper

Threads & Needles

See page 22.

CUTTING OUT

See the liftout sheet for the pattern and embroidery designs. See page 104 for the cutting layouts.

Cut two rectangles from the linen and two from the interfacing, each 32cm x 35cm wide (12 1/2" x 13 3/4") for the front pocket and the back of the bag. The pieces will be cut to their exact shape after the embroidery is complete.

Trace the remaining pattern pieces for the bag and lining onto tracing paper.

PREPARATION FOR EMBROIDERY

Fuse the interfacing to the wrong side of each corresponding rectangle of linen.

Using a pen, trace the pattern pieces for the front pocket and for the back of the bag, including the embroidery designs, onto tracing paper. Cut out the tracings along the marked cutting lines.

Transferring the designs

Place the pocket tracing onto the right side of the pocket rectangle, aligning the placement marks with the straight grain of the fabric. Pin in place to prevent movement. Draw around the pattern piece.

Place a piece of the transfer paper, colour side down, onto the fabric between the fabric and the tracing. Pressing firmly, trace over a small section of the embroidery design with the ball point pen. Carefully lift the traced section to check that it is transferring onto the fabric. If the marks are faint press more firmly. Mark the outlines for the ribbon, stems and large leaves. Trace the circles for the large roses and the shapes for the rosebuds. Mark the centres of the rosettes and the clematis with small dots. Transfer the pattern shape and the embroidery design for the back of the bag in the same manner.

EMBROIDERY

See page 23 for the step-by-step instructions for rosette stitch.

Use the milliner's needle when stitching the bullion knots, the crewel needle when stitching with two strands and the sharp needle when stitching with one strand of thread.

Stolen sweets are always sweeter, stolen kisses much completer,
stolen looks are nice in chapels, stolen, stolen, be your apples.

LEIGH HUNT. SONG OF FAIRIES ROBBING AN ORCHARD

Order of work

Work the design on the front pocket piece first. The embroidery on the back is stitched in a similar manner to the front.

Ribbon

The twisting ribbon is embroidered as a foundation over which the sprays of flowers trail. Outline the ribbon with stem stitch, then embroider closely packed rows of stem stitch to fill the ribbon shapes.

Large roses

To embroider the large roses refer to the photograph on the previous page for colour and petal placement. For the centre of each rose, work two bullion knots in the darkest pink thread. Surround these with inner petals, stitching between three and five bullion knots in the medium pink thread. Add one to four outer petals to all the roses except the rose at the base of the design. This rose has a centre and inner petals only.

Work a calyx at the base of each rose with two bullion knots placed beside the outer petals. Stitch a third bullion knot at the centre of the calyx on two of the roses at the base of the design.

Large rosebuds

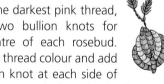

Using the darkest pink thread, work two bullion knots for the centre of each rosebud. Change thread colour and add a bullion knot at each side of the centre. Work the calyx in the same manner as the roses, placing a third bullion knot in the centre of some buds.

Small rosebuds

Stitch two tapered bullion knots for each bud and add a green bullion knot each side for the calyx.

Large rose foliage

Work the leaves in fly stitch, starting each one at its tip, stitching towards the base. Add the stems in stem stitch.

Clematis

Stitch the darker mauve clematis first. Where necessary, stitch on top of the foundation stem stitch ribbon. Each flower is formed with four granitos petals. Use four stitches to work each granitos. Change to the lighter mauve thread and embroider the remaining flowers in each group.

Work the stems in stem stitch and add the leaves with detached chains.

Climbing rose

Embroider each stem with a single row of stem stitch, stitching the stems so that they appear to go over and under the foundation ribbon. For the rose trailing below the design, thicken the base of the main stem.

Taper back to one row halfway along the stem's length. Leaves embroidered in detached chain, each with a long anchoring stitch are then placed randomly along the stems. Following the step-by-step instructions work the three clusters of rosette stitch roses. Embroider the tiny buds in French knots, sprinkling them among the leaves.

"THERE IS NO NEED TO RIGIDLY FOLLOW MY DESIGN. TO ACHIEVE YOUR OWN LOOK, VARY THE POSITIONS OF THE FLOWERS AND LEAVES."

Kris

CONSTRUCTION

See pages 104 - 107.

THREADS

Madeira stranded cotton

A = 0808 vy lt antique mauve

B = 0809 med antique violet

C = 0810 vy dk antique violet

D = 1508 dk green-grey

E = 1903 vy dk beige-grey

F = 2114 dk golden olive

Anchor stranded cotton

G = 269 ultra dk avocado green

H = 869 vy lt antique violet

I = 870 lt antique violet

J = 892 ultra lt shell pink

NEEDLES

No. 1 milliner's needle

No. 8 crewel needle

No. 12 sharp needle

Nan's Apple Pie Recipe

2 sheets of shortcrust pastry

FILLING

1 1/4 kg golden delicious apples, peeled, cored and cut into thick slices

50g preserved ginger, cut into small pieces

1/2 cup brown sugar

1 tablespoon lemon juice

2 teaspoons ground cinnamon

1/2 teaspoon ground nutmeg

METHOD

Pre-heat the oven to 230°C. Line a pie dish with one sheet of the pastry. Mix together all the filling ingredients. Place in the pie dish. Cut the remaining piece of pastry into 1/2 inch strips. Arrange the strips in a crisscross pattern over the pie. Trim and crimp the edges. Bake for 20 minutes then reduce the heat to 190°C and continue to cook for a further 40 minutes. Serve the pie warm with a dollop of cream.

EMBROIDERY KEY

All embroidery is worked with one strand of thread unless otherwise specified.

Ribbon = F (stem stitch)

Large roses

Centre = C (3 strands
2 bullion knots, 10 wraps)

Inner petals = B (3 strands
3 - 5 bullion knots, 15 - 20 wraps)

Outer petals = A (3 strands
1 - 4 bullion knots, 15 - 20 wraps)

Calyx = D (3 strands, 1 - 3 bullion
knots, 10 - 12 wraps)

Large rosebuds

Centre = C
(3 strands, 2 bullion knots, 10 wraps)

Outer petals = B
(3 strands, 2 bullion knots, 10 wraps)

Calyx = D
(3 strands, 2 - 3 bullion knots, 8 wraps)

Small rosebuds

Bud = B or C
(3 strands, 2 bullion knots, 10 wraps)

Calyx = H
(3 strands, 2 bullion knots, 8 wraps)

Large rose foliage

Leaves = D (fly stitch)

Stems = D (stem stitch)

Clematis

Flowers = H or I (2 strands granitos)

Stems = E (stem stitch)

Leaves = E (detached chain)

Climbing roses

Stems = G (stem stitch)

Leaves = G (detached chain)

Rose petals = J (2 strands, rosette stitch)

Rose centre = A
(2 strands, French knot, 2 wraps)

Tiny buds = A
(2 strands French knot, 2 wraps)

ROSETTE STITCH ROSE

Rosette stitch roses are a quick and effective way to add variety to floral embroidery. The needle is inserted into the fabric to form the framework around which the thread is wound. After winding, the thread is couched in place.

We used no. 5 perlé cotton for photographic purposes only.

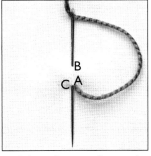

1. Bring the needle to the front at A. Insert needle at B, 2 - 3mm (1/8") above A. Re-emerge at C, left of A. Leave needle in fabric.

2. Pick up the thread at A. Wrap the thread under each end of the needle in an anti-clockwise direction.

3. Work 2 - 3 more wraps in the same manner. Ensure the wraps lie side-by-side and not on top of each other.

4. Holding the wraps in place with your left thumb near the top, gently pull the needle through.

5. Still holding the wraps with your thumb, take the thread over the wraps and to the back of the fabric.

6. Pull the thread through. Bring the needle to the front at the top, just inside the last wrap.

7. Take the needle to the back just over the last wrap and pull the thread through.

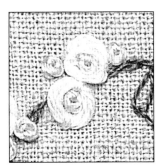

8. Embroider a two wrap French knot in the centre. **Completed rosette stitch rose.**

SPRING
BOUQUET

PRETTY AND FUNCTIONAL.
THE PERFECT GIFT.

BY ANGELA WATSON

THE FAIRY FLOWER

THE HONEYSUCKLE IS SAID TO BE A FLOWER OF THE FAIRIES, ITS INTOXICATING SCENT
STRONGEST AT NIGHTFALL. A YOUNG MAN COULD ENCOURAGE A GIRL TO DREAM
PASSIONATELY ABOUT HIM BY REPEATING HIS NAME THREE TIMES OVER A POSY MADE OF
HONEYSUCKLE. HE THEN HAD TO STEAL INTO HER ROOM, IN ORDER TO PLACE THE POSY
NEAR HER BED, SO THAT AS SHE SLEPT SHE WOULD BREATHE IN THE HEADY SCENT.

This very feminine and romantic cosmetic purse is made from ivory damask, generously decorated with a spray of roses and a sprinkling of delicate flowers.

REQUIREMENTS

Fabric

45cm x 50cm wide (17 3/4" x 19 3/4") piece of ivory damask

30cm x 45cm wide (11 3/4" x 17 3/4") piece of calico for lining the purse

15cm x 35cm wide (6" x 13 3/4") piece of ivory moiré for lining and binding the tissue holder

Supplies

30cm x 45cm wide (11 3/4" x 17 3/4") piece of thin wadding eg Pellon

55cm x 20mm wide (21 5/8" x 3/4") ivory bias binding

25cm (10") ivory zip

6mm (1/4") linking brass ring

20mm (3/4") brass ring

15cm (6") embroidery hoop

Sharp HB pencil

Threads, Beads & Needles

See page 29.

PREPARATION FOR EMBROIDERY

See the liftout sheet for the patterns and embroidery designs. See page 107 for the cutting layouts.

Large spray on cosmetic purse

Cut a piece of damask, 45cm x 28cm wide (17 3/4" x 11") for the purse. This will be cut to the exact shape after the embroidery is complete.

Using a black pen, trace the purse pattern piece and embroidery design onto tracing paper. Tape the tracing to a window or lightbox. With the right side of the fabric facing you, place the fabric over the tracing allowing extra fabric to extend beyond the pattern piece at the end to be embroidered. This will allow the embroidery to be worked in the hoop. Tape in place. The light shining through will make the design easier to see. Using the lead pencil, trace the cutting lines and embroidery design onto the damask. Remove the tape and damask.

Small spray on purse tab

Cut a piece of damask, 10cm x 22cm wide (4" x 8 5/8") for the zip tab. This will be cut to the exact shape after the embroidery is complete.

Trace the tab pattern piece and embroidery design onto tracing paper and tape it to a window or lightbox in the same manner as before. Centre the damask over the pattern piece. Tape the fabric in place and trace the cutting lines and embroidery design in the same manner as the purse front.

Sprays on tissue holder

Use the remaining piece of damask for the tissue holder. This will be cut to the exact shape after completing the embroidery.

Transfer the marked cutting lines and embroidery designs in the same manner as the previous pieces, ensuring the pattern piece is centred.

"THE COSMETIC PURSE AND TISSUE HOLDER ARE NOT ONLY PRACTICAL BUT WOULD MAKE A LOVELY GIFT FOR A SPECIAL FRIEND. MOST OF MY EMBROIDERY WORK INCLUDES RIBBON, BUT I DECIDED TO USE THREADS ONLY FOR THESE ITEMS SO THEY CAN BE LAUNDERED WITHOUT RUINING ANY OF THE EMBROIDERY."

Angela

THIS DESIGN USES

Beading · Bullion knot
Colonial knot · Couching
Detached chain · Grab stitch
Granitos · Fly stitch
Smocker's knot · Straight stitch

THE FINISHED COSMETIC PURSE MEASURES 15.5 x 21cm WIDE (6" x 8 1/4")
THE FINISHED TISSUE HOLDER MEASURES 9cm x 13.5cm WIDE (3 1/2" x 5 1/4")

EMBROIDERY

See page 29 for step-by-step instructions for fly stitch.

Use the no. 7 milliner's needle for stitching the bullion knots, the no. 9 milliner's needle for stitching the colonial knots and the beading needle for attaching the glass flowers and beads. The crewel needle is used for all other embroidery.

Place the purse and tissue holder fabric in the hoop for all embroidery except the bullion knots. The embroidery on the purse tab is not worked in the hoop.

Order of Work

Large spray on cosmetic purse

Stitch the roses first using three bullion knots for the centre of each rose and six to seven bullion knots for the petals. Embroider four small rosebuds around the roses. Add a large rosebud above the central rose. For this bud embroider a straight stitch on each side for the sepals and a grab stitch around the base of the bullion knots.

Work a pair of detached chain leaves on the stem of each rosebud and add two groups of detached chain leaves to the upper bullion rose. Embroider the large fly stitch leaves next. Use six to seven fly stitches for each one and finish with a smocker's knot at the base of the last fly stitch.

Add straight stitch stems to the leaves, then couch the longer stems in place.

Stitch three forget-me-nots on each side of the roses. To create the petals, work five narrow fly stitches with very short anchoring stitches around the marked centre. Work a single straight stitch inside each fly stitch. Add a colonial knot to the centre.

Embroider the lilac next, forming each flower with a granitos of five straight stitches. Surround the lower half of each flower with a fly stitch and work a straight stitch from the centre of the flower to the base, to form the sepals. Work loose straight stitches for the stems, shaping them into curves before couching in place.

Work the honeysuckle in the same manner as the lilac flowers. Surround the lower half of each flower with a fly stitch for the sepals.

Randomly scatter pink colonial knots around the roses and blue-violet colonial knots around the forget-me-nots for the scattered buds.

Finally attach the two glass flowers. Take the needle up through the centre of the flower, attach a gold bead and take the needle back down through the centre.

Small spray on purse tab

Stitch the large bullion rose in a similar manner to those on the purse. Add a group of three detached chain leaves on each side of the rose.

Embroider four lilac flowers, two on each side of the rose. Stitch the flower heads and sepals in the same manner as those on the purse but do not add the stems. Using the darker pink thread, scatter eight tiny colonial knot buds around the spray.

Sprays on tissue holder

The two floral sprays on the tissue holder are almost identical. For each spray embroider the rose first, followed by the rosebud. Work the rosebud with two bullion knots side by side for the centre. Beginning at the base each time, stitch two shorter bullion knots for the inner petals. Surround the lower half of the bud with a long curved bullion knot for the outer petals. Add two detached chains for the sepals and a straight stitch stem and leaves to the rosebud on one design.

Work three detached chain leaves around each rose. Stitch the large leaves, forget-me-not, lilac and honeysuckle in the same manner as those on the front of the purse.

CONSTRUCTION

See pages 107 - 109.

"A TRAVELLING PACK OF TISSUES FITS IN THE TISSUE HOLDER"

Angela

THREADS, BEADS AND NEEDLES

Madeira stranded cotton

A = 0813 shell pink

B = 0814 lt shell pink

C = 0901 lt blue-violet

D = 1511 vy lt fern green

E = 2013 lt tan

F = 2110 vy lt verdigris

G = 2207 vy lt old gold

H = 2611 vy lt antique violet

Mill Hill petite glass beads

I = 40557 gold (2 beads)

Mill Hill glass treasures

J = 12149 blue flowers (2 flowers)

Needles

No. 7 crewel embroidery

No. 7 milliner's

No. 9 milliner's

No. 10 beading

EMBROIDERY KEY

All embroidery is worked with two strands of thread unless otherwise specified.

Large spray on cosmetic purse

Roses

Centre = A (3 bullion knots 6 - 7 wraps)

Petals = B (6 - 7 bullion knots 10 - 12 wraps)

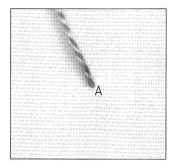

Small rosebuds

Petals = A (2 bullion knots 8 wraps)

Sepals = D (straight stitch, grab stitch)

Large rosebud

Centre = A (2 bullion knots 8 wraps)

Outer petals = B (2 bullion knots 7 wraps)

Sepals = D (straight stitch, grab stitch)

Leaves and stems

Large leaves = D (fly stitch, smocker's knot)

Stems to large leaves = D (straight stitch, couching)

Small leaves = D (detached chain)

Forget-me-nots

Petals = C (fly stitch straight stitch)

Centre = G (colonial knot)

Lilac

Flowers = H (granitos)

Sepals = D or F (1 strand, fly stitch, straight stitch)

Stems = D or F (1 strand, straight stitch, couching)

Honeysuckle

Flowers = E (granitos)

Sepals = F (fly stitch)

Glass flowers = I and J (beading)

Scattered buds = B and C (1 strand, colonial knot)

Small spray on purse tab

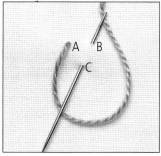

Rose

Centre = A (3 bullion knots, 6 - 7 wraps)

Petals = B (8 bullion knots, 10 - 12 wraps)

Leaves = D (detached chain)

Lilac

Flowers = H (granitos)

Sepals = F (1 strand, fly stitch straight stitch)

Scattered buds = A (1 strand colonial knot)

Sprays on tissue holder

Rose

Centre = A (3 bullion knots 6 - 7 wraps)

Petals = B (8 - 9 bullion knots 10 - 12 wraps)

Rosebud

Centre = A (2 bullion knots 8 wraps)

Inner petals = B (2 bullion knots, 8 wraps)

Outer petal = B (bullion knot, 12 wraps)

Sepals = D (detached chain)

Stems = D (straight stitch)

Leaves and stems

Large leaves = D (fly stitch smocker's knot)

Stems to large leaves = D (straight stitch)

Small leaves = D (detached chain)

Forget-me-nots

Petals = C (fly stitch straight stitch)

Centre = G (colonial knot)

Lilac

Flowers = H (granitos)

Sepals = F (1 strand fly stitch, straight stitch)

Stems = F (1 strand, straight stitch couching)

Honeysuckle

Flowers = E (granitos)

Sepals = D (fly stitch)

FLY STITCH

Fly stitch is an open detached chain stitch with many possible variations.
It is worked in the shape of a 'V' or 'Y' depending on the length of the anchoring stitch.

1. Bring the thread to the front at A. This will be the left hand side of the stitch.

2. Take the needle to the back at B and re-emerge at C. Loop the thread under the tip of the needle and to the right.

3. Hold the loop in place under the left thumb (thumb not shown). Pull the needle through until the looped thread lies snugly against C.

4. Take the thread to the back at the required distance below C to anchor the fly stitch. **Completed fly stitch.**

Sunbury
Racing Club.

Grand Ball,
PROGRAMME.

Mechanics'
Institute
Sunbury..

Lyceum Wh___

SOLE LESSEE AND MANAGER

MR. HENRY IRVING.

BECKE___

88TH TO 92ND PERFORMANCES

The Fifteenth Season of the present M___

EVENING
WEDNESDAY, JANUARY

A 6
STALLS 3/-

__UARY 10th

BLUE DANUBE

by Anna Scott

"The handbag has faithfully mirrored women's occupations and aspirations.
On the one hand, bags are entirely practical and on the other
they are the stuff of fantasy..."

FROM A CENTURY OF BAGS: ICONS OF STYLE IN THE TWENTIETH CENTURY, BY C WILCOX

Twilight on a warm summer evening is reflected in the colours and blooms of this stylish little handbag. The bead embroidery is worked using simple stitches with the sparkle of Marguerite crystals highlighting the larger flowers.

REQUIREMENTS

Fabric

40cm x 75cm wide (14 3/4" x 29 1/2") piece of jacaranda silk dupion

25cm x 50cm wide (10" x 20") piece of ivory silk lining

Supplies

40cm x 75cm wide (14 3/4" x 29 1/2") piece of medium weight woven fusible interfacing

40cm x 75cm wide (14 3/4" x 29 1/2") piece of shapewell

20cm (8") jacaranda zip

Jacaranda sewing thread

20.5cm x 4cm (8 1/8" x 1 1/2") piece of template plastic

Tissue paper

Sharp HB pencil

Threads, Beads & Needles

See page 35.

THIS DESIGN USES

Attached bead, Beaded back stitch
Couched beads, Lazy squaw stitch
Couched lattice

PREPARATION FOR EMBROIDERY

See the liftout sheet for the embroidery design and pages 109 - 110 for the cutting layout and preparing the silk for beading.

The silk is backed with interfacing and mounted onto shapewell before commencing the embroidery. Neaten the raw edges of the front piece with a machine zigzag or overlock stitch to prevent fraying.

All beading and embroidery is worked before cutting out the exact shape.

Transferring the design

Using a pen, trace the cutting lines, design and placement marks onto the tissue paper. Centre the tissue paper over the front piece of the bag, aligning the placement marks on the design with the straight grain of the fabric. Pin in place. Using contrasting sewing thread, work small tacking stitches along the cutting lines, stem lines and outlines of the larger flowers. Using the pencil, pierce the tissue paper and mark the centre of all flowers.

Gently score the tissue paper with a blunt needle, then carefully remove the paper.

EMBROIDERY

See page 35 for step-by-step instructions for beaded back stitch.

Use the crewel needle for the embroidery and the beading needle for all beading.

Order of work

Branch

Embroider the couched lattice over the branch. Bead the outline of the branch after all the flowers have been worked.

Large cream flowers

Attach the silver Marguerite crystal in the centre of the flower with an aurora bead.

Thread sixteen mardi gras red beads onto the needle. Take the needle through the first bead of the row to make a circle *(diag 1)*.

Diag 1

Place the circle around the centre crystal and, using the same thread, couch in place between every second bead.

Back stitch nine rose beads along each vein following the step-by-step instructions.

Diag 2

Back stitch a row of eleven cream beads on either side of each vein curving at the tip, leaving a space at the point *(diag 2)*.

Thread back through one side of cream beads, from the flower centre to the tip. Attach a single bead between the rows at the tip and thread the other side *(diag 3)*.

Diag 3

Bead the outline of the petals in a similar manner. Bead the remaining two cream flowers in a similar manner using sufficient beads to cover the outlines.

THE FINISHED BAG MEASURES 14.5cm x 20.5cm WIDE (5 3/4" x 8 1/8")

Purple flowers

Attach a Marguerite crystal at the centre of a purple flower in the same manner as before.

Bead the outline of the petals in a similar manner to the large cream flowers, using salmon beads. Fill each petal with rows of purple beads across the petal, fitting snuggly between the outlines.

Work the remaining three purple flowers in the same manner.

Small blossoms

For each blossom, attach a single rose bead at the centre.

Thread seven cream beads and make a circle in the same manner as the centre of the large cream flowers. Couch the circle in place around the centre bead.

Branch

Work the outline of the branch using beaded back stitch, leaving the section at the lower right hand corner until after the bag is complete.

CONSTRUCTION

See pages 109 - 111.

THREADS, BEADS AND NEEDLES

Au Ver à Soie, Soie d'Alger
A = 1736 vy dk slate blue

Maria George glass seed beads
B = 6110 aurora

Maria George lustre seed beads
C = 7019 purple

Maria George antique seed beads
D = 9142 peacock
E = 9153 salmon

Mill Hill glass seed beads
F = 00123 cream (2 pkts)
G = 00553 old rose

Mill Hill antique seed beads
H = 03058 mardi gras red

Marguerite 6mm crystals
I = silver (7 crystals)

Needles
No. 9 crewel
No. 10 bead embroidery

EMBROIDERY KEY

All embroidery is worked using one strand. All beading is worked with doubled sewing thread.

Branch = A (lattice couching)
D (beaded back stitch)

Large cream flowers = B and I (attached bead), H (couched circle)
F and G (beaded back stitch)

Purple flowers = B and I (attached bead), E (beaded back stitch), C (lazy squaw stitch)

Small blossoms = G (attached bead)
F (couched circle)

BEADED BACK STITCH

Beaded back stitch is used to cover smooth curves and long lines.

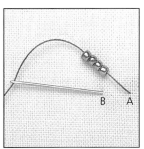

1. Bring needle to the front at A. Thread four beads onto the needle and insert it at B.

2. Bring the needle to the front between the second and third bead.

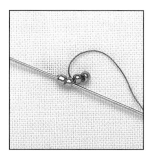

3. Take the needle through beads 3 and 4.

4. Thread two beads onto the needle and insert it at C.

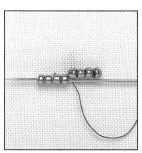

5. Repeat steps 2 - 4 until the row is complete.

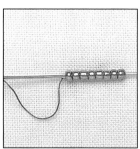

6. Bring needle to the front at end. Thread back through the entire row. Take to the back. Secure.

SUMMER FRUIT

"This wonderful project allows

you to explore stumpwork and

raised embroidery techniques

on a large scale. Working with

yarn, threads and beads, the

embroidery is easy to see and

grows quickly."

BY JAN KERTON

All needleworkers love bags for projects and precious treasures, so Jan has designed a pretty and practical damask drawstring work bag. Two external pockets are decorated with beautiful raised berry sprays. You may wish to decorate one, two or all four pockets.

REQUIREMENTS

Fabric

84cm (33") square of ivory damask

84cm x 115cm wide (33" x 45 1/4") calico

25cm (10") square of red homespun

5cm x 8cm wide (2" x 3") piece of white wool felt

5cm x 8cm wide (2" x 3") piece of black wool felt

6cm x 16cm wide (2 3/8" x 6 1/4") piece of red wool felt

4cm (1 1/2") square of white organza for bee's wings

Supplies

15cm x 60cm wide (6" x 23 1/2") piece of interfacing

1m x 23mm wide (39 1/2" x 7/8") green satin ribbon

6cm x 13cm wide (2 3/8" x 5") piece of appliqué paper

Small amount of polyester fibre-fill

15cm (6") embroidery hoop

Sharp HB pencil

Fray stopper

Fine paintbrush

Threads, Beads & Needles

See page 44.

CUTTING OUT

See page 111 for the cutting layouts.

Using the pencil, rule a 30.5cm (12") square in each corner of the ivory damask. The distance between the squares is 23cm (9"). Cut out the squares leaving a cross shaped piece of fabric for the bag *(diag 1)*. The four squares will be used for the outer pockets.

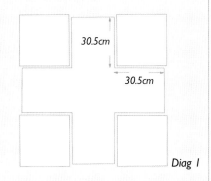

Diag 1

Cut out the calico for the lining to the same measurements. The four calico squares will be used for the pockets inside the bag.

Cut two extra pieces of calico, each 30.5cm (12") square to stabilise the embroidered areas.

PREPARATION FOR EMBROIDERY

See the liftout sheet for the embroidery designs.

Marking the design placements

Fold one pocket square of damask in half and press. The fold will become the upper edge of the pocket. Unfold the damask fabric. Mark the centre of the fold line with a pin. Repeat the procedure on one more square of damask.

Transferring the designs

Cut two pieces of interfacing, each 12cm x 16cm wide (4 3/4" x 6 1/4"). Trace the embroidery designs onto the pieces of interfacing using a black pen. Tape one tracing to a window or light box. Place one of the marked squares of damask over the tracing so the fold line and the pin on the fabric are aligned with the placement marks on the tracing. Tape in place to prevent movement. The light shining through will make the design easier to see through the fabric. Using the pencil, transfer the design onto the damask fabric.

Transfer the remaining design to the second marked piece of damask in the same manner.

> "I HAVE EMBELLISHED MY BERRY SPRAY WITH A BEE, SPIDER, SNAIL AND LADYBIRD. HOWEVER, YOU CAN ADD A TOUCH OF INDIVIDUALITY BY STITCHING YOUR OWN INSECTS AND GARDEN CREATURES."
>
> Jan

Transferring the berry shapes

Trace the six berry shapes onto a piece of interfacing. Using the pencil, transfer the raspberry and blackberry shapes onto the red homespun, using the same method as the designs on the damask. Ensure the shapes are within the boundary of the hoop.

Preparing the pocket piece

Pin one square of calico onto the wrong side of one prepared damask pocket panel. Baste around the edges or overlock the two pieces together. Repeat for the second pocket panel to be embroidered.

EMBROIDERY

See pages 46 - 47 for step-by-step instructions for working needlewoven bars and the berry tassels. See the liftout sheet for the embroidery designs and templates for the berries and insects. See page 45 for instructions to make a twisted cord.

All embroidery is worked with the fabric in the hoop, except for the bullion knots and cast-on stitch.

Both designs are worked in a similar manner with the exception of the tiny garden creatures and the spent raspberry flower which features on the design with the bee and snail.

Order of work

Strawberry leaves

Using the no. 24 chenille needle, embroider the outline of the leaves in holbein stitch. Keep the stitches approximately 2 - 3mm (1/8") long. Work the vein of each leaf.

Embroider straight stitches for padding inside the leaf shapes. Place the stitches in a brick pattern, making them longer on the right side of the work than on the wrong side *(diag 2)*.

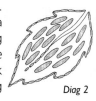

Diag 2

Begin the blanket stitch at the base of one leaf by working a detached chain from the vein to the edge of the leaf. Anchor the detached chain by working a blanket stitch beside it.

Continue working with slanted blanket stitches up to the tip of the serration, pulling the stitches tight and flat. Work the stitches close together and follow the outline of the leaf.

"TO MAKE THE TIP LOOK MORE DEFINED, FINISH THE LAST BLANKET STITCH WITH A LONG ANCHOR STITCH. IF YOU HAVE TO JOIN IN A NEW THREAD, FINISH AT THE TIP AND START THE NEW THREAD IN THE DIP."

Jan

Start the new serration with a detached chain in the 'dip'.

When you have stitched approximately two thirds of the tip of the leaf, gradually alter the angle of the stitches so they eventually point towards the tip *(see diag 3)*.

Work the other side of the leaf in the same manner, covering the vein line *(diag 3)*.

Diag 3

Embroider the remaining leaves in the same manner.

Using the yellow-green wool and starting at the base of the stem, work stem stitch along the right hand side of the stem up to the base of the middle leaf. Continue along the leaf's vein line working one third of the way into the leaf.

Change to the light pistachio green wool and work a line of stem stitch close to the previous row, working two to three longer stitches along the tip of the vein line.

Continuing with the same wool, start at the base of the stem and work stem stitch close to the previous row up to the base of the left leaf. Change to the yellow-green wool and work two to three longer stitches along the vein line of the left leaf. Finish with two to three stitches in light pistachio green from the base of the leaf along the vein line.

Using the yellow-green wool, start at the base of the right leaf and work in a similar manner along the vein line. Finish with two to three stitches in light pistachio green from the base along the vein line.

Work two double detached chains 1cm (3/8") long to form the calyx at the base of the stem.

Strawberry stems

Cut two pieces of wool, each 1.2m (1yd 11") in length and make a twisted cord following the instructions on page 45.

Thread the unknotted end of the cord into the no. 20 chenille needle and bring the cord to the front of the fabric at the start of the stem line. Using matching green sewing thread and the no. 9 crewel needle, couch the cord along the marked stem. Ensure the couching stitches are concealed within the twists of the cord. Take the cord through to the back of the fabric at the end of the stem. Trim the cord, leaving a 6mm (1/4") tail. Secure the tail to the calico with the couching thread, ensuring no stitching shows on the right side of the fabric.

Knot the end of the cord again and repeat for the remaining stems, working the strawberry stem last. Leave the twisted cord dangling on the right side at the base of the strawberry for the sepals.

Strawberry bud

Embroider the bud at the end of the left stem using a granitos of three to four straight stitches.

Small strawberry nodes

Remove the fabric from the hoop and work two small nodes at the point where the stems divide. Use approx-imately fifteen cast-ons for each one.

Strawberry flower

Trace the flower shape onto the backing of the appliqué paper. Fuse the flower shape to the white felt. Carefully cut out the flower. Peel away the paper backing and place the flower into position with the adhesive side on the fabric. Pin in place. Work a small holding stitch at the tip of each petal. Remove the pin. Use the tip of the iron to fuse the flower into position.

Using the pencil, mark the flower centre with a circle. Back stitch around the circle with white sewing thread. Using the pale lemon yarn, satin stitch the flower centre.

Satin stitch over the white felt to form the petals. Work single detached chains between the petals. Attach the gold beads around the edge of the flower centre.

Strawberry

Trace the strawberry shapes onto the appliqué paper and fuse to the red felt in the same manner as the strawberry flower. Carefully cut out the shapes and then peel away the paper backing.

With the fusible side down, place the smallest shape in the centre of the strawberry outline. Catch into position in four places using small stitches. Place the middle sized shape over the smallest shape, fusible side down. Catch into position as before. Place the largest shape over the previous shapes and catch into position.

Blanket stitch around the outer edge of the strawberry shape. Starting at the tip of the strawberry and keeping the stitches quite long, stitch three detached chains. Anchor the stitches at the tip *(diag 4)*. Work the next row of detached chains in the gaps between the first three stitches, ensuring they overlap. Continue stitching in the same manner until three quarters of the strawberry is covered.

Diag 4

Work the remaining stitches radiating from the base *(diag 5)*. This gives more of a three dimensional look to the fruit. Using the antique gold metallic thread, embroider small straight stitches over the anchoring stitch of the detached chains for the seeds.

Diag 5

THIS DESIGN USES

Back stitch

Beading

Blanket stitch

Bullion knot

Cast-on stitch

Couching

Detached chain

French knot

Granitos

Holbein stitch

Long and short stitch

Needlewoven bar

Needlewoven open base picot

Padded satin stitch

Running stitch

Satin stitch

Straight stitch

Stem stitch

Strawberry sepals

Using the dangling twisted cord make four loops, each 8mm (5/16") long. Couch them to the base of the strawberry. Take the remaining cord through to the back of the fabric and secure it firmly with the couching thread.

Raspberry and blackberry stems

Cut two pieces of light pistachio green wool, each 1.2m (1yd 11") in length. Knot the ends together. Make a twisted cord and attach to the design in the same manner as the strawberry stems.

Blackberry leaf

Outline the leaf and vein in holbein stitch. Using the darker green yarn and angling the stitches toward the tip, work long and short stitch along both sides of the leaf vein. Vary the length of the stitches as you work. Change to the light pistachio green yarn. Stitch the remainder of the leaf in a similar manner, working from the leaf edge to the darker green stitching. Using the mocha thread, finish with large back stitches along the main vein and straight stitches for the smaller veins.

"THE COLOURS SHOULD BLEND. ADD EXTRA KNOTS IF NECESSARY TO ACHIEVE THIS EFFECT. MAKE SURE THE KNOTS ARE PACKED TOGETHER FIRMLY, AS THEY WILL OPEN OUT MORE WHEN THE BERRY IS FORMED."

Jan

Lower raspberry

Place the red cotton fabric in the hoop. Using two strands of Q, work French knots at one end of the berry shape. Fill one third of the shape. Dot a few single knots further out so the colours will blend. Change to one strand each of O and Q blended together. Continue working French knots in the same manner for a further one third of the shape. Change to two strands of O and continue to fill the shape. Attach beads among the French knots.

Upper raspberry

Embroider this berry in a similar manner to the lower berry, changing the colour of the wools for each quarter. Use two strands of Q for the lower quarter. Change to O and Q for the next quarter and to O for the third quarter. Work the final quarter with N and O. Add the beads as before.

Blackberry

Work French knots to cover the berry shape. Attach beads on top of the French knots, covering the entire shape. Randomly mix the bead colours.

Applying the berries

Stitch a line of running stitch 2mm (1/8") away from the edge, around each of the berries, leaving tails of thread at the beginning and end. Cut out the shape of the berry approximately 2mm (1/8") from this line of stitching. Pull up the running stitch tightly and tie off. You will have little embroidered berry shapes.

Place the berries in position on the damask. Secure with stab stitches under the edge.

Raspberry sepals

Using the no. 24 tapestry needle, work a needlewoven bar 1cm (³⁄₈") long for the first sepal. Take the needle to the back of the fabric at the base of the bar so it forms a loop. Work three more bars at the base of the raspberry, varying the lengths and angles of the bars. Work needlewoven bars for the remaining raspberries.

Blackberry sepals

Work three to four needlewoven open base picots at the base of the blackberry. Manipulate each picot into the desired position and anchor with tiny stitches.

Spent raspberry flower

Using the crewel needle, work six straight stitches and attach a petite bead at the tip of each stitch for the stamens. Embroider three sepals at the base in the same manner as the raspberry sepals. Couch the two side sepals into position.

Spent blackberry flower

Stitch five needlewoven picots in a circular shape. Work three tiny straight stitches radiating from the base on each picot for sepal markings. Attach one bead in the centre of the flower and then surround this with seven beads placed in a circle.

Side view spent blackberry flower

Work four to five straight stitches, attaching a petite bead at the tip of each stitch for the stamens. Embroider two to three picots for the sepals. Couch into place.

Snail

The shell is formed with a forty wrap bullion loop. Bring the thread to the front at the opening of the shell. Take the needle from the centre of the shell to where it previously emerged, ready to work the wraps.

Stitch the bullion loop and twist into a spiral. Pull tightly on the thread to help set the shape of the shell. Take the needle to the back of the fabric at the centre of the shell. Couch the shell into position.

Work the body with a single bullion knot. Pull tightly so that the bullion narrows towards the tail. Add two straight stitches for the feelers.

> "TO VARY THE LOOK OF YOUR SNAIL, YOU CAN BLEND A NUMBER OF SHADES TOGETHER TO FORM A MORE MOTTLED COLOUR FOR THE SHELL."
>
> Jan

Bee

Embroider the legs with straight stitches. Work six bullion knots for the abdomen. Begin near the thorax with a yellow knot and alternate the yellow and black knots until reaching the tip of the abdomen.

Trace the wing shape onto the organza and cut out. Using a fine paintbrush, dab a little fray stopper on the edges of both wings. Centre the wings over the thorax and secure the middle with black thread. Fill the thorax area with padded satin stitch. Work a single bullion knot for the head and then work two straight stitches for the feelers.

Ladybird

Trace the body onto appliqué paper. Fuse the paper to the red felt and carefully cut out the body shape. Position it on the strawberry leaf and fuse in place. Completely cover the felt with satin stitch. Work a straight stitch down the centre of the body to divide the wings and embroider a French knot spot on each wing. Stitch the head with a bullion knot and the feelers and legs with straight stitches.

Spider and web

Work each of the spokes of the web with long straight stitches and add two stitches across the top. Stitch two rounds of the web, taking a tiny back stitch over each spoke. Keep the thread above the needle for each stitch.

Attach a bead for the spider's body and a smaller one for its head. Embroider the legs in back stitch, passing the needle under the beads.

Strawberry Tassel

Trace the strawberry shape on the liftout sheet onto the interfacing and cut out. Pin the shape to the red felt and cut out. Make the strawberry tassel following the step-by-step instructions on page 47.

Blackberry Tassel

Cut the blackberry shape from the black felt in the same manner as for the strawberry. Make the blackberry tassel following the step-by-step instructions on page 47.

CONSTRUCTION

See pages 111 - 113.

THREADS AND BEADS

DMC stranded cotton

A = 310 black
B = 321 vy lt garnet
C = 407 mocha
D = 522 fern green (2 skeins)
E = 712 cream
F = 927 lt grey-green

DMC broder médicis

G = 8102 burgundy
H = 8103 med red
I = 8369 lt pistachio green
J = 8406 pistachio green
K = 8407 dk blue-green
L = 8420 yellow-green
M = 8748 pale lemon

Appletons 2 ply crewel wool

N = 352 vy lt grey-green
O = 946 dk bright rose pink
P = 992 off-white
Q = 995 cherry red

Mill Hill antique glass beads

R = 3034 amethyst

Mill Hill glass seed beads

S = 00367 garnet
T = 02014 black

Mill Hill petite glass beads

U = 42011 Victorian gold
V = 42014 black (1 bead)
W = 42028 ginger

Kreinik metallics Balger cord

X = 105 antique silver
Y = 205 antique gold

EMBROIDERY KEY

All embroidery is worked with one strand unless otherwise specified.

Strawberry leaves

Outline = J (holbein stitch)

Padding = J (straight stitch)

Leaf = J blended with K
(1 strand of each, blanket stitch)

Stem and vein = I and L
(stem stitch)

Calyx = J blended with K (1 strand of each, double detached chain)

Strawberry stems

Twisted cord = I and L
(1 strand of each, twisted cord)
machine sewing thread (couching)

Strawberry bud = I blended with L (1 strand of each, granitos)

Strawberry nodes = I
(cast-on stitch)

Strawberry flower

Centre = M (satin stitch)
U and E (beading)

Petals = P (satin stitch)
L (detached chain)

Strawberry

Berry = B (straight stitch blanket stitch), G blended with H (1 strand of each, detached chain)

Seeds = Y (straight stitch)

Sepals = I and L (1 strand of each, twisted cord), machine sewing thread (couching)

Blackberry and raspberry stems

= I (2 strands, twisted cord)
machine sewing thread (couching)

NEEDLE CHART

NO. 10 BEADING *Beading*

NO. 9 CREWEL *1 strand of thread*

NO. 20 CHENILLE *Twisted cord*

NO. 22 CHENILLE *2 strands of wool*

NO. 24 CHENILLE *1 strand of wool*

NO. 24 TAPESTRY *Needlewoven bar, Needlewoven open based picot*

NO. 1 MILLINER'S *Bullion knot, Cast-on stitch, French knot*

Blackberry leaf

Outlining and padding = I (holbein stitch)
J and I (long and short stitch)
C (back stitch, straight stitch)

Raspberry

Lower berry = Q (2 strands French knot, 1 wrap)
O blended with Q (1 strand of each, French knot, 1 wrap)
O (2 strands, French knot 1 wrap), B (running stitch straight stitch) B, R and X (beading)

Upper berry = Q (2 strands, French knot, 1 wrap), O blended with Q (1 strand of each, French knot, 1 wrap), O (2 strands French knot, 1 wrap), N blended with O (1 strand of each, French knot, 1 wrap), B (running stitch straight stitch), B, R and S (beading)

Sepals = J (needlewoven bar)

Spent raspberry flower

Flower = C (straight stitch)
C and U (beading)

Sepals = J (needlewoven bar)

Blackberry

Berry = A (3 strands, French knot 1 wrap), A, S and T (beading)
A (running stitch, straight stitch)

Sepals = I (needlewoven open base picot)

Spent blackberry flower

Petals = I (needlewoven open base picot)

Petal markings = C (straight stitch)

Centre = C and W (beading)

Side view spent blackberry flower

Petals = I (needlewoven open base picot)

Stamens = C (straight stitch)
C and W (beading)

Snail

Shell = C (6 strands, bullion loop 40 wraps), C (couching)

Body = F (3 strands, bullion knot, 20 wraps)

Feelers = F (straight stitch)

Bee

Legs = A (straight stitch)

Abdomen = A and M (3 strands 6 bullion knots, 5 - 9 wraps)

Thorax = A (2 strands padded satin stitch)

Head = A (2 strands, bullion knot 8 wraps)

Feelers = A (straight stitch)

Ladybird

Body = G (satin stitch)
A (straight stitch)

Spots on wings = A (French knot 2 wraps)

Head = A (bullion knot, 12 wraps)

Legs and feelers = A (straight stitch)

Spider's web = X (straight stitch back stitch)

Spider

Body = A and T (beading)

Head = A and V (beading)

Legs = A (back stitch)

Berry Tassels

Strawberry = G blended with H (1 strand of each, detached chain)
B and U (beading)

Sepals = I (needlewoven open base picot)

Blackberry = A (3 strands French knot, 1 wrap) A, S and T (beading), A (running stitch straight stitch)

Sepals = I (needlewoven open base picot)

Twisted cord = D (6 strands twisted cord)

MAKING A TWISTED CORD

A twisted cord is used for the berry stems and the drawstring in *Summer Fruit*. We used a tool called a spinster to make our twisted cord.

1. Cut strands of yarn or thread of the required length. Fold in half to double the number of strands.

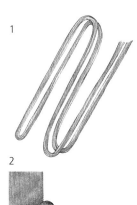

2. Knot the ends together and hook the loop of the folded end over a door handle.

3. Hook the knotted end onto the hook of the spinster.

4. Keeping threads taut, turn them in a clockwise direction until the twist has the desired tension.

5. Bring the two ends together, holding at the halfway point.

6. Keeping twisted threads fully stretched, release 10cm - 15cm (4" - 6") at a time until all the cord is twisted.

7. Remove the loop from the door knob and knot the ends together.

N E E D L E W O V E N   B A R

Needlewoven bars make realistic sepals or tiny leaves.
One end of each needlewoven bar is detached from the fabric.
The bar can then be gently manipulated and the free end anchored to the fabric.
We used no. 5 perlé cotton for photographic purposes only.

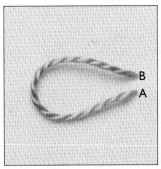

1. Secure the thread on the back. Bring the thread to front at A and take to back at B, leaving a loop of thread approx. 10mm (³/₈") long on the front.

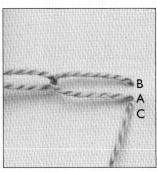

2. Re-emerge at C, just below A taking care not to pull the loop through. Pass a piece of waste thread through the loop.

3. With your left hand, hold the waste thread taut, slightly above the surface of the work. Continue to hold this taut while you work.

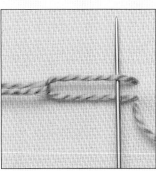

4. Weave the needle over the lower thread of the loop and under the upper thread. Do not pierce the fabric.

5. Pull the thread through firmly and push the wrap down onto the fabric with the tip of the needle.

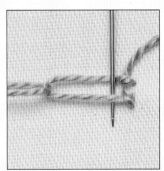

6. Weave the needle over the upper thread and under the lower thread. Do not pierce the fabric.

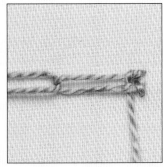

7. Pull through firmly and push the wrap down the loop with the tip of the needle so it sits snugly against the first wrap.

8. Continue working steps 4 - 7, weaving the stitches over and under the threads of the loop. Push each wrap firmly against the previous one.

9. Continue weaving until the loop is completely filled and the wraps are firmly packed.

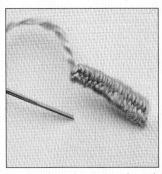

10. Remove the waste thread. Take the needle to the back. Vary the position of the needle to suit the design.

11. Pull thread through. The bar curls and twists, giving a three dimensional effect. **Completed needlewoven bar.**

12. The green sepals below the raspberries and the spent raspberry flower are formed with needlewoven bars.

MAKING THE STRAWBERRY TASSEL

1. Cut out the strawberry shape. Fold the felt shape at the centre so the straight side comes together to form a cone.

2. Whip the edges of the felt together with B and turn to the other side.

3. Using the no. 22 chenille needle and one strand each of G and H, work detached chains from base of the strawberry to within 12mm (1/2") of top edge.

4. Work running stitch around the top edge. Fill with fibre-fill and pull up the stitches firmly. Back stitch to finish off the thread.

5. Stitch detached chains around the top of the berry, radiating the stitches from the gathered centre.

6. Attach tiny gold beads (U) over the surface for seeds.

7. Work six picots at the top for sepals. Adjust the tip of each picot evenly. Anchor with tiny stitches.

8. Attach the strawberry firmly to the twisted cord. **Completed strawberry tassel.**

MAKING THE BLACKBERRY TASSEL

1. Cut out the shape. Stitch around the curve to form a cup. Turn to the other side. Gather, fill and secure.

2. Cover the entire shape with beads (S and T). Mix the beads, selecting them at random.

3. Work four picots at the top for sepals. Adjust the tip of each picot and anchor with tiny stitches.

4. Attach the blackberry firmly to the twisted cord. **Completed blackberry tassel.**

IN THE VICTORIAN 'LANGUAGE OF FLOWERS' THE STRAWBERRY REPRESENTS 'PERFECT EXCELLENCE'.

FRESH FIELDS

by Joan Gibson

Featuring a selection of enchanting country garden flowers, this versatile bag would be perfect for holding everyday essentials when shopping. Quick and easy to make, the bag would also be ideal to carry delicious picnic provisions.

REQUIREMENTS

Fabric

55cm x 140cm wide (22" x 55") blue and cream striped cotton

38cm x 32cm wide (15" x 12 5/8") piece of cream homespun

Supplies

35cm x 112cm wide (13 3/4" x 44") medium weight interfacing

12cm (5") embroidery hoop

Sharp HB pencil

Threads & Needles

See page 51.

PREPARATION FOR EMBROIDERY

See the liftout sheet for the embroidery design.

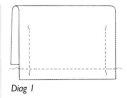

Diag 1

Measure up 3cm (1 1/4") from the lower edge of the homespun and stitch a row of tacking parallel to the edge of the fabric. Measure in 3cm (1 1/4") from each side and tack in the same manner for 18cm (7") *(diag 1)*.

Transferring the design

Position the homespun over the embroidery design, aligning the tacked lines with the placement lines on the design. Using the pencil, trace the design onto the fabric.

EMBROIDERY

Use the hoop when working the sunflowers, cornflowers, poppy centres, buds and centres of the daisies. Bind the inner ring with cotton tape or bias binding ironed flat.

The milliner's needle is used for the ears of wheat, the no. 7 crewel needle when working the sunflower petals, the tapestry needle for whipping and the no. 9 crewel needle for all other embroidery.

Order of work

Sunflowers

Petals

Embroider each petal, working three straight stitches into the same two holes in the fabric. Vary the length of the petals so that some are longer than others.

Centre

Fill the inner circle with tightly packed green French knots. Using the beige thread, fill the remainder of the centre in the same manner.

Stems

Embroider the main stems, then those of the leaves in stem stitch. Whip the main stems, taking the needle under every stem stitch *(diag 2)*.

Diag 2

Leaves

To achieve the curled effect at the tip of the leaf, work the first fly stitch longer on one side, curling the long side of the stitch to the left or right *(diag 3)*.

Continue working close fly stitches to complete each leaf. Finish the base of each leaf with two to three straight stitches.

Diag 3

Poppies

Flower

Embroider a blanket stitch pinwheel for the facing blooms and a partial blanket stitch pinwheel for the side view blooms. The remaining flowers are stitched in two parts. Work the area closest to the stem first. Begin the remainder of the flower as shown in diagram 4. Fill the centres with closely packed French knots.

Diag 4

Buds and foliage

Work the stems in stem stitch, then each small bud with a granitos that has been padded with several horizontal straight stitches. Begin each leaf at the base. Work stem stitch along the centre, making the last stitch longer than the previous stitches. Add pairs of straight stitches along the stem stitch, angling them towards the tip of the leaf.

Cornflowers

Foliage

Stitch the stems and large leaves first, followed by the calyxes. At the top of each stem, work three to five horizontal straight stitches for padding. Cover these with a layer of vertical satin stitches. Embroider three tiny stem stitches for each small leaf.

Facing flowers

Work four straight stitches for the petals, leaving a space in the centre *(diag 5)*. Stitch three to five petals of varying lengths in each quarter space. Using the black thread, embroider nine to eleven straight stitches over the blue petals and in the spaces between. Take these stitches slightly further into the centre than the blue stitches.

Diag 5

Back view flower

Work petals of varying lengths and angles from the top of the calyx.

Ears of wheat

Work the stems first and then the leaves. Stitch the grains next, starting with the single bullion at the top, then in pairs. Finish with a long straight stitch at the tip of each bullion for the whiskers.

Daisies

Flowers

Work detached chain stitches for the full and partial flowers, leaving a space in the centre. Fill the centres of the flowers with French knots.

Foliage

Work the stems in stem stitch and the small leaves with two small straight stitches for each leaf. For each larger leaf, embroider a detached chain. Surround it with a second detached chain.

THIS DESIGN USES

Blanket stitch · Bullion knot
Detached chain · Fly stitch
French knot · Granitos
Padded satin stitch · Stem stitch
Straight stitch
Whipped stem stitch

THREADS AND NEEDLES

DMC stranded cotton

A = blanc

B = 310 black

C = 320 med pistachio green

D = 471 vy lt avocado green

E = 666 bright Christmas red

F = 729 med old gold

G = 733 med olive green

H = 743 yellow

I = 792 dk cornflower blue

J = 841 lt beige

K = 989 vy lt forest green

L = 3363 med pine green

Needles

No. 7 crewel

No. 9 crewel

No. 9 milliner's

No. 24 tapestry

EMBROIDERY KEY

All embroidery is worked with two strands unless otherwise specified.

Sunflowers

Petals = H (3 strands straight stitch)

Centre = E (French knot 1 wrap), J (French knot, 2 wraps)

Main stems = L (whipped stem stitch)

Leaf stems = L (stem stitch)

Leaves = L (fly stitch, straight stitch)

Poppies

Petals = E (blanket stitch)

Centre = B (French knot, 2 wraps)

Stems = C (1 strand, stem stitch)

Buds = C (1 strand, granitos)

Leaves = C (stem stitch straight stitch)

Cornflowers

Petals = I (straight stitch)

Petal markings = B (1 strand, straight stitch)

Calyx = K (1 strand padded satin stitch)

Stems = K (1 strand, stem stitch)

Large leaves = K (1 strand, stem stitch)

Small leaves = K (1 strand, straight stitch)

Ears of wheat

Stems = F (1 strand, stem stitch)

Grains = F (7 - 9 bullion knots, 9 wraps)

Whiskers = F (1 strand, straight stitch)

Leaves = F (1 strand, stem stitch)

Daisies

Petals = A (detached chain)

Centre = H (French knot, 2 wraps)

Stems = D (1 strand, stem stitch)

Small leaves = D (1 strand, straight stitch)

Large leaves = D (detached chain)

CONSTRUCTION

See pages 113 - 114 for preparing the embroidery. See pages 52 - 53 for step-by-step instructions for constructing the bag.

No, the heart that has truly lov'd never forgets, But as truly loves on to the close,
As the sunflower turns on her god, when he sets, The same look which she turn'd when he rose.

THOMAS MOORE

CAREFUL CONSTRUCTION WILL ENSURE THAT YOUR BAG LASTS FOR MANY YEARS.

MAKING THE BAG

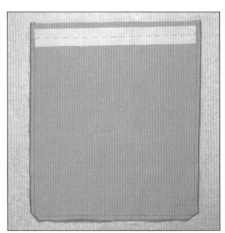

1. Cut two strips of interfacing, fold in half along the length. Tack each strip along the top of each fabric piece.

2. With right sides together, pin and stitch the front to the back, leaving the top open. Clip the corners and neaten the seams.

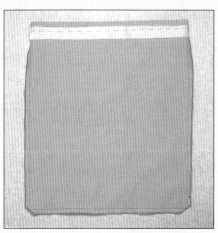

3. Turn in 1cm (³/₈") along the raw edge of the fabric and press.

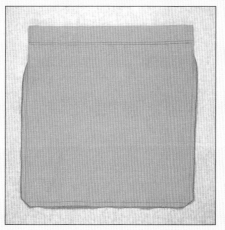

4. At the top edge, measure down 4cm (1 ½"). Fold to the wrong side and press. Stitch in place. Remove tacking.

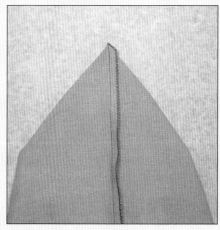

5. Forming the base. Fold the lower seam to align with the side seam.

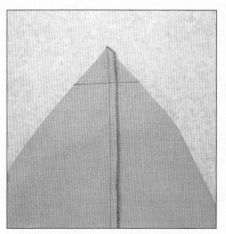

6. Stitch across each corner 4.5cm (1 ³/₄") from the point. This will box form the base of the bag. Do not trim.

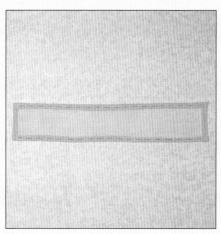

7. Lay each strip of interfacing over each handle strip. Turn in 1cm (³/₈") along each long edge. Press and tack.

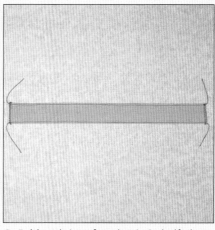

8. Fold each interfaced strip in half along the length and tack. Top stitch along each long edge. Neaten the raw ends. Remove the tacking.

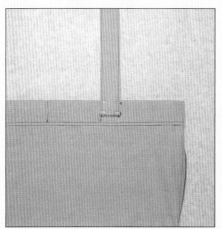

9. Measure 4.5cm (1 ³/₄") on each side of the centre and mark with a pin. Align the inner handle edge to the bag, allowing 2.5cm (1") to overlap inside the bag.

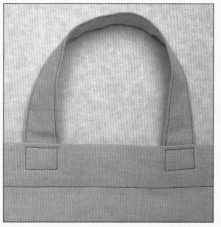

10. Stitch around each end of the handle to attach it to the bag. Repeat for the remaining handle.

CELADON

An exquisite willow green evening bag lavishly embroidered with
sparkling beads and lustrous threads by Anna Scott.

T he beautiful blooms of the exotic pink peony decorate the front of this silk evening bag. Rows of beads in shades of soft pink are stitched to form the petals of the open flowers and buds. The large leaves are embroidered in satin stitch and the veins, smaller leaves and sepals are worked in beads.

REQUIREMENTS

Fabric

25cm x 90cm wide (10" x 35 1/2") piece of willow green shot silk dupion

25cm x 60cm wide (10" x 23 1/2") piece of ivory silk lining

Supplies

25cm x 60cm wide (10" x 23 1/2") piece of medium weight woven fusible interfacing

25cm x 60cm wide (10" x 23 1/2") piece of shapewell

4.5cm x 18cm wide (1 3/4" x 7") piece of template plastic

65cm (25 1/2") of size 6 piping cord

Fine white beading thread

Tracing paper

Carbon paper

Fine black pen

Beads, Threads & Needles

See page 57.

PREPARATION FOR EMBROIDERY

See the liftout sheet for the embroidery design. See page 114 for the cutting layouts and preparing the silk for beading.

The silk is backed with interfacing and mounted onto shapewell before the embroidery is commenced. Neaten the raw edges of the front piece with a machine zigzag or overlock stitch to prevent fraying.

Transferring the design

Using the pen, trace the design and placement marks onto the tracing paper. Centre the tracing over the front piece of the bag. Pin in place.

Slide the sheet of carbon paper between the tracing and the fabric, with the carbon side facing the silk.

Retrace the design using a ball-point pen.

EMBROIDERY

See the liftout sheet for the stitch direction diagram.

Use the crewel needle for the embroidery and the bead embroidery needle for all of the beading.

Start and finish the beading thread with a smocker's knot on the reverse side of the embroidery.

Order of work

Stems

Bring the needle to the front at one end of a stem. Thread on enough bugle beads to loosely cover the length of the stem.

Take the needle to the back at the end of the stem and work a couching stitch between each bugle.

Repeat for the remaining stems.

Small leaves

Outline the leaves with light grey-green beads. Couch a row of ice green beads along the centre vein of each leaf *(diag 1)*.

Diag 1

Large leaves

Outline the leaves with split back stitch. Work long straight stitches as padding along the length of each leaf.

Cover the leaves with satin stitch, bringing the needle up outside the outline and down through the centre vein of the leaf.

THE FANCIFUL BLOOM OF THIS BEADED BAG WAS INSPIRED BY A JAPANESE PRINT.

THE FINISHED BAG MEASURES 18cm x 22cm WIDE (7" x 8⅝")

Work a row of back stitch along the centre vein, spacing the stitches and threading a light grey-green bead onto each stitch *(diag 2)*.

Diag 2

Flowers

Outline the front petal of each flower with dusty rose beads. Fill the petal with old rose beads, placing rows across the petal *(diag 3)*.

Diag 3

Outline the centre of each flower and cover with padded satin stitch.

Outline the remaining petals and fill each, referring to the photograph for colour placement.

Randomly scatter a mix of yellow and gold beads above each flower.

Buds

Outline each petal with dusty rose beads and fill with rows of beads along the length of each petal.

Randomly scatter a mix of yellow and gold beads below each bud.

Sepals

Fill the sepals under each bud with rows of beads placed side-by-side across each sepal.

CONSTRUCTION

See pages 114 - 115.

THIS DESIGN USES

Attached bead
Back stitch beading
Beaded outline stitch
Couched beads
Lazy squaw stitch
Padded satin stitch
Split backstitch

BEADS, THREADS AND NEEDLES

Maria George Delica beads

A = DBR 233 lined crystal/yellow lustre

B = DBR 675 satin blush white

C = DBR 689 semi-matte silver lined light grey-green

Mill Hill glass seed beads

D = 00553 old rose

E = 00561 ice green

F = 02005 dusty rose

G = 02011 Victorian gold

H = 02012 royal plum

3mm bugle beads

I = emerald

Caron collections 'Waterlilies' stranded silk

J = 106 olive

Madeira stranded silk

K = 2013 lt tan

Needles

No. 9 crewel

No. 10 bead embroidery

EMBROIDERY KEY

All embroidery is worked with one strand. All beading is worked with doubled beading thread.

Foliage

Stems = I
(couched beads)

Small leaves = C
(beaded outline stitch)
E (couched beads)

Large leaves = J (split back stitch padded satin stitch)
C and J (beaded back stitch)

Flowers

Front petals = F (beaded outline stitch), D (lazy squaw stitch)

Centre = K (split back stitch padded satin stitch)
A and G (attached beads)

Side petals = B (beaded outline stitch), D and F (lazy squaw stitch)

Buds

Petals = F (beaded outline stitch)
D and H (lazy squaw stitch)
A and G (attached beads)

Sepals = E (lazy squaw stitch)

HOME COMING

by Susan O'Connor

Lavish wool cashmere velour roses and leaves adorn the lower edge of this striking bag.

REQUIREMENTS

Fabric

20cm x 95cm wide (8" x 37 ½") piece of black wool cashmere velour

20cm x 150cm wide (8" x 59") piece of red wool cashmere velour

25cm x 30cm wide (10" x 11") piece of olive wool cashmere velour

20cm x 65cm wide (8" x 25 ½") piece of red polyester satin

Supplies

20cm x 45cm wide (8" x 17 ¾") piece of black lightweight woven fusible interfacing

18cm (7") square of buckram

White chalk based fabric marker

No. 5 crewel needle

PREPARATION

See page 115 for the cutting layouts. See the liftout sheet for the leaf template.

CONSTRUCTION

See page 115.

WOOL CASHMERE VELOUR LEAVES

Use the leaf template on the liftout sheet for creating the four wool leaves. Contrasting thread has been used for photographic purposes only.

1. With wrong sides together, fold the olive cashmere in half along the length. Using the fabric marker, trace four leaf shapes onto the right side of the cashmere.

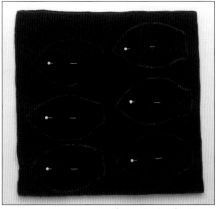

2. Pin the centre of each leaf shape through both layers of the fabric to secure.

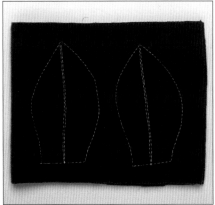

3. Using matching machine sewing thread, sew around the leaf outline. Stitch two rows for the leaf vein through the centre of the shape.

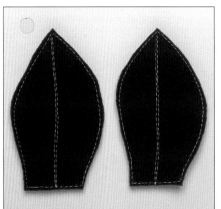

4. Cut out the leaf shape close to the stitching. **Completed leaves.**

F O L D E D   W O O L   C A S H M E R E   V E L O U R   R O S E S

Wool cashmere velour is ideal for making the roses as it does not fray. Make nine roses.

1. Trim one end of the wool strip diagonally as shown.

2. Holding the length of fabric horizontally, fold the right end over aligning the diagonal with the lower raw edge.

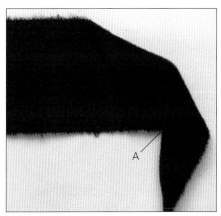

3. Fold the point until the folded edge meets at A.

4. Fold again to the left, meeting the edge of the fabric at B. Stitch through all layers to secure. Do not finish off.

5. First petal. Holding the centre in your right hand, fold the top edge of the fabric back and down with your left hand.

6. Roll the centre onto the folded fabric, pick up your dangling needle and stitch through all layers at the base.

7. Second petal. Fold the top edge of the fabric back and down as before. Following step 6, roll the centre onto the folded fabric and secure the second petal.

8. Final petal. Fold the fabric back and down and secure as before.

9. Finish the last petal by folding the tail and tapering it towards the base. Secure in place. Trim the excess fabric.

ALL ROSES

by Kris Richards

Kris has designed this superb little handbag using her beautiful roses and buds. The subtle texture of the cream furnishing fabric is brought to life with trailing blooms, sprays of tiny flowers and delicately shaded hydrangeas.

REQUIREMENTS

Fabric

40cm x 95cm wide (15 3/4" x 37 3/8") piece of cream medium weight furnishing fabric

40cm x 95cm wide (15 3/4" x 37 3/8") piece of calico

Supplies

40cm x 95cm wide (15 3/4" x 37 3/8") piece of lightweight fusible wadding eg. Pellon

25cm x 16cm wide (10" x 6 1/4") piece of template plastic

15cm (6") diameter rattan handles

Tissue paper

Sharp HB pencil

Threads & Needles

See page 65.

PREPARATION FOR EMBROIDERY

See the liftout sheet for the pattern and embroidery design. See page 116 for the cutting layout.

From the furnishing fabric, cut a 35cm (14") square for the front of the bag. All embroidery is worked before cutting out the exact shape of the front.

Transferring the design

Using the pencil, trace the cutting lines, design and placement marks onto the tissue paper. Place the tissue paper over the fabric, aligning the placement marks on the design with the straight grain of the fabric. Pin in place. Using contrasting sewing thread, work small tacking stitches along the stem lines. Using the pencil, pierce the tissue paper and mark the centre of each rose and hydrangea with a dot. Mark the pink and lavender sprays and cream flowers in a similar manner. Work small tacking stitches along the cutting lines.

Lightly moisten the tissue paper with a damp sponge, wait a few seconds, then carefully remove the paper.

EMBROIDERY

Use the milliner's needle when working the roses and hydrangeas and the crewel needle for all other embroidery.

Order of work

Stems

With two stands of thread, embroider the stems in stem stitch.

Roses

The roses and rosebuds vary in colour and size. Refer to the close-up photograph for placement.

Full blooms

There are two colour combinations, each combination using three of the four shades of pink.

For the centre of each rose, work two bullion knots in the darkest shade. Surround these with two or three inner petals in the medium shade (*diag 1*).

Diag 1

With the lightest shade, add three or four outer petals (*diag 2*).

Diag 2

Large rosebud

Embroider the largest bud at the centre top of the design using three of the shades of pink.

Small rosebuds

Embroider these in a similar manner, working a long anchoring stitch on one centre bullion. Refer to the photograph for the number of petals in each bud.

For the sepals of the rosebuds, work a fly stitch around the base of the bud and add three bullion knots, curving them around or away from the bud and anchoring with a long stitch (*diags 3 and 4*).

Diag 3   *Diag 4*

Leaves

Using the photograph for placement, embroider the large leaves surrounding the roses in fly stitch. Begin each one at its tip and work towards the base (*diag 5*).

Diag 5

Changing to the lighter shade of green, add the pairs of small detached chain leaves, working a long anchoring stitch at the tip of each leaf.

Hydrangeas

With six strands of thread, work tightly packed French knots. Begin at the centre of the flower, working towards the outer edge. Layer the knots in the centre to create a rounded flower.

Work fly stitch leaves and add pairs of detached chain leaves as before.

Pink and lavender sprays

Embroider the stems and work the rosette stitch flowers. Add the tiny buds with French knots and stitch the detached chain leaves.

Daisies

Small daisies are scattered around the centre of the design, subtly adding texture. Embroider four granitos petals for each flower, each with four straight stitches worked into the same two holes (*diag 6*).

Diag 6

CONSTRUCTION

See pages 115 - 117.

THIS DESIGN USES

Bullion knot · Detached chain
Fly stitch · French knot · Granitos
Rosette stitch · Stem stitch

THREADS AND NEEDLES

Anchor stranded cotton

A = 387 stone
B = 854 taupe
C = 870 lt antique violet
D = 892 ultra lt shell pink
E = 893 vy lt shell pink
F = 894 lt shell pink
G = 896 dk shell pink

Finca stranded cotton

H = 5156 dk fern green
I = 5236 dk khaki green
J = 8599 vy lt antique violet

*Needle Necessities
stranded variegated cotton*

K = 141 Spanish moss
L = 149 hydrangea

Needles

No. 1 milliner's
No. 8 crewel

EMBROIDERY KEY

*All embroidery is worked with two
strands unless otherwise specified.*

Roses

Stem = H (stem stitch)

Full blooms

Centre = F or G (6 strands
2 bullion knots, 8 wraps)

Inner petals = E or F (6 strands
2 - 3 bullion knots, 12 wraps)

Outer petals = D or E (6 strands
3 - 4 bullion knots, 15 wraps)

Large rosebud

Centre = G
(4 strands, bullion knot, 12 wraps)

Inner petals = F
(4 strands, 2 bullion knots, 15 wraps)

Outer petals = D (4 strands
3 bullion knots, 15 wraps)

Sepals = H (3 bullion knots, 10 wraps)

Small rosebuds

Centre = E, F or G
(4 strands, 1 or 2
bullion knots, 12 wraps)

Petals = D, E or F (4 strands
2 bullion knots, 12 wraps)

Sepals = H (fly stitch
3 bullion knots, 10 wraps)

Stem = H (stem stitch)

Leaves = H (fly stitch), B (detached chain)

Hydrangeas

Flowers = K and L
(6 strands, French knot)

Leaves = I (fly stitch)
B (detached chain)

Pink and lavender sprays

Stems = H and I
(stem stitch)

Petals = D or J
rosette stitch)

Centre = C or E
(French knot, 2 wraps)

Buds = C or E
(French knot, 2 wraps)

Leaves = I (detached chain)

Daisies = A (granitos)

VINTAGE
by Judy Stephenson

~ THE WONDROUS ART OF CASALGUIDI ~

Casalguidi embroidery appears to have its origins in the late nineteenth century in a small village in Italy bearing the same name. This style of embroidery is a form of whitework, traditionally involving fabric which has been spun or woven from flax fibres. The use of colour is now an accepted addition.

The form and texture of the raised embroidery is perfectly framed by the counted stitchwork of the border, decorative side seams and edging. The twisted cord is held by neat blanket stitch loops and is finished with beautifully decorated tassels. The traditional monotone of the chosen threads serves to concentrate the eye on the beauty and form of the embroidery.

REQUIREMENTS

Fabric
50cm x 25cm wide (19 3/4" x 10") piece of cream 25 count Lugana linen
50cm x 25cm wide (19 3/4" x 10") piece of ivory satin

Supplies
10cm (4") square of cream felt
30cm x 5cm wide (12" x 2") piece of medium weight non-woven interfacing
Small amount of fibre-fill
20cm (8") embroidery hoop
11 x 8mm (5/16") natural colour wooden beads
Tracing paper
Sharp HB pencil

Craft Smart Off'n On glue
Wooden skewer

Threads & Needles
See page 71.

PREPARATION FOR EMBROIDERY
See the liftout sheet for the embroidery design.

Preparing the fabric
When cutting the fabric to size, cut between the threads to keep the fabric square. Neaten all edges with a machine zigzag or overlock stitch. Turn each short end under 2cm (3/4") and tack firmly. Do not turn the sides under until the embroidery on the front is complete.

Fold the fabric in half across the width and work a row of tacking along the foldline with the machine sewing thread. This line represents the lower edge of the bag.

Divide the front into quarters. Work lines of horizontal, then vertical tacking, beginning at the centre. Tack four threads under, then four threads over, to facilitate placement of the four sided stitch *(diag 1)*. The lines of tacking remain in place until all embroidery is complete.

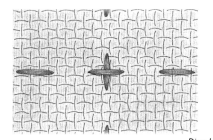

Diag I

Transferring the design
Using a black pen, trace the design onto the tracing paper. Tape the tracing to a window or light box.

With the right side up, place the prepared fabric over the tracing, aligning the tacking lines with the placement marks. Tape in place. The light shining through will make the design easy to see. Using the pencil, trace the design.

THIS DESIGN USES
Back stitch · Blanket stitch
Buttonhole edging · Couching
Detached blanket stitch
Double blanket stitch
Four sided stitch
Italian insertion stitch · Satin stitch
Stem stitch · Tassel making
Twisted cord · Wrapping

"I FIND THIS STYLE OF EMBROIDERY VERY EXCITING BECAUSE IT COMBINES THE DISCIPLINE OF COUNTED STITCHWORK AS EVIDENCED IN THE FOUR SIDED STITCH FRAMEWORK, WITH THE ELEMENTS OF FREE FLOWING RAISED DESIGN DEMONSTRATED IN THE BRANCH, LEAF AND GRAPES. I AM INDEBTED TO EFFIE MITROFANIS FOR THE HISTORY AND DIVERSE TECHNIQUES CONTAINED IN HER BOOK CASALGUIDI STYLE LINEN EMBROIDERY."

Judy

EMBROIDERY

See pages 73-75 for step-by-step instructions for working a grape, raised stem stitch branch and Italian insertion stitch side seams. See pages 117-118 for the tassel.

The embroidery design is worked with the fabric in the hoop.

Use the tapestry needle when working with the perlé cottons and when working the detached blanket stitch and the stem stitch on the branch. Use the milliner's needle for all other embroidery.

Order of work

Border

Work the border of the design in four sided stitch. Begin with the longest row, two threads from the vertical centre tacked line and sixty-two threads up from the horizontal tacked line. Work one four sided stitch over the centre block of four threads, then work sixteen on each side of the centre, making thirty-three in all. Repeat on the remaining three sides.

Begin and end the second row at the top, four blocks in from each end of the first. Work two more rows in the same manner. Repeat on the remaining three sides.

To create the raised effect, thread the tapestry needle with a 60cm (24") length of C and, leaving a short tail, bring the thread to the front inside the first four sided stitch of the long row (diag 2).

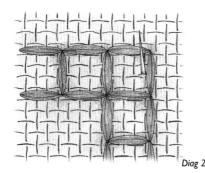

Diag 2

Take the thread under the vertical loops of the four sided stitch along the row. At the end of the row, take the thread to the back just inside the last stitch. Re-emerge next to the first stitch of the next side of

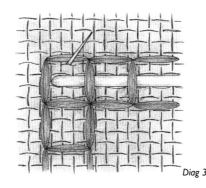

Diag 3

the border (diag 3). Continue as before, working the thread under the vertical stitches on each side. When all four sides are complete, secure the two ends of thread carefully at the back.

Run the thread under the remaining rows of four sided stitch, securing the tails of thread at the beginning and end of each row.

Vine

Branch

Embroider the branch following the step-by-step instructions.

Leaf

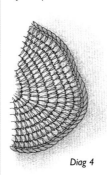

Diag 4

Outline the leaf shape with back stitch. Work blanket stitch over the back stitch, ensuring the stitches are not too wide or too tight. Changing thread and needle, work detached blanket stitch to fill one section of the leaf shape (diag 4). When the first section is complete, push a small amount of fibre-fill under the detached blanket stitch. Continue covering the leaf shape in the same manner, padding each section as you complete it. Referring to the

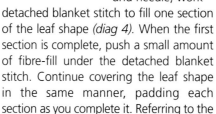

Diag 5

photograph for placement, lay down lengths of four strands of B for the veins. Wrap each vein with two strands of the same thread (diag 5).

Couch in place with one strand.

Leaf stem

Anchor four 15cm (6") lengths of the padding thread on the back of the fabric at the top of the leaf. Bring the threads to the front and take them over the branch, draping them loosely, before securing on the back of the fabric (diag 6).

Diag 6

Bring the wrapping threads to the front in the same manner as the padding and wrap the padding closely (diag 7). Adjust the wrapping and placement of the stem before securing the wrapping threads on the back as before.

Diag 7

Diag 8

Work a loop of padding threads over the branch for the next section of the stem (diag 8).

Wrap in the same manner as before. For the last section of the stem, lay the padding threads in the same manner, wrapping more tightly towards the end to give a tapered effect. Couch in place.

Grapes

Make the eleven grapes following the step-by-step instructions, and attach them to the fabric at the marked positions.

Work the stem in the same manner as the stem of the leaf.

Tendrils

The tendrils are created in the same manner as the stems, using the ecru stranded cotton.

Decorative side seams

Remove the fabric from the hoop. Turn each side of the fabric under 2cm (3/4") and tack firmly.

The strip of interfacing is used as a guide or spacer when joining the side seams with the Italian insertion stitch.

Draw two parallel lines down the centre of the interfacing, 5mm (³/₁₆") apart. Work the insertion stitch following the step-by-step instructions.

Loops

The cord is held by five loops on the front of the bag and five on the back. Work the centre front loop first. Count up sixteen threads along the central line of tacking

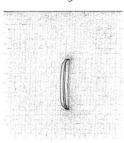

Diag 9

from the top row of four sided stitch. Make a loop from this point over the next twelve threads by stitching twice with D *(diag 9)*.

With the same thread, work double detached blanket stitch over the two strands. Use two needles to do this, one each side of the loop, and alternate the stitches *(diag 10)*.

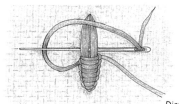

Diag 10

Work the next two loops 3cm (1¹/₄") in from the sides of the bag. The remaining two loops are evenly spaced between these three.

Decorative upper edge

Use the tapestry needle to work the blanket stitch scalloped edge. Beginning at a side seam, work a loop over the insertion stitch *(diag 11)*.

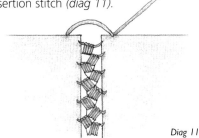

Diag 11

Lay the thread loosely along the top and catch the fabric nine threads further along, anchoring with a tiny stitch *(diag 12)*.

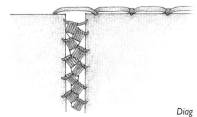

Diag 12

Continue in this manner until nearing the starting point. Check the number of threads remaining so that the loops can be adjusted if necessary to keep them as even as possible.

Work eight blanket stitches into each loop. Form the scallop by taking the ninth stitch through the fabric at the point where the loop is attached.

Change to three strands of B and work a second row of blanket stitch.

Cords and tassels

Make the two twisted cords and tassels following the instructions on page 118.

CONSTRUCTION

See page 118.

THREADS & NEEDLES

DMC stranded cotton

A = ecru (2 skeins)

B = 3033 vy lt putty groundings (2 skeins)

DMC no. 5 perlé cotton

C = ecru

DMC no. 8 perlé cotton

D = ecru

Needles

No. 5 milliner's

No. 24 tapestry (2 needles)

EMBROIDERY KEY

All embroidery is worked with one strand unless otherwise specified.

Border = D (four sided stitch) C (threading)

Vine

Branch = D (padding), A (2 strands couching, 3 strands, straight stitch) B (3 strands, satin stitch, 3 strands stem stitch)

Leaf

Outline = B (3 strands back stitch, blanket stitch)

Filling = D (detached blanket stitch)

Veins = B (4 strands, laid thread 2 strands, wrapping, couching)

Stems = D (4 strands, padding) A (4 strands, wrapping)

Grapes = A (2 strands, blanket stitch, detached blanket stitch)

Tendrils = A (3 strands, padding 2 strands, wrapping)

Decorative side seams = D (Italian insertion stitch)

Loops = D (double blanket stitch)

Decorative upper edge = C (blanket stitch), B (3 strands, blanket stitch)

Cord = A

Tassel

Skirt = C

Head = A (3 strands, detached blanket stitch), B (3 strands detached blanket stitch, double detached blanket stitch)

We are born at a given moment,
in a given place and, like vintage years of wine,
we have the qualities of the year
and of the season of which we are born.

CARL JUNG, SWISS PSYCHIATRIST

GRAPE

Each grape is worked with two strands of thread, each 1m (39") in length.
It is important to have enough thread to finish the grape without having to join it.

1. Wrap the threads twice around the skewer, leaving a 12cm (4 ¾") tail.

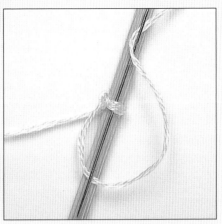

2. Leaving the tail dangling, work blanket stitch over the threads to form a ring.

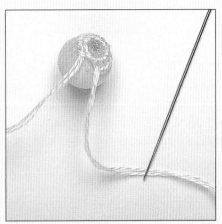

3. Put a small amount of glue on the top of a bead. Wait until it is tacky and place the ring over it.

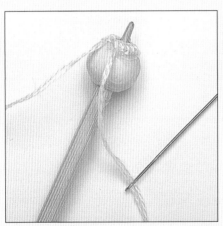

4. Insert the pointed end of the skewer into the hole at the base of the bead.

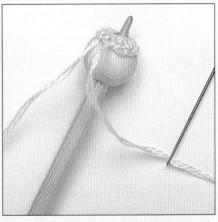

5. Begin working detached blanket stitch into the ring, covering the tail.

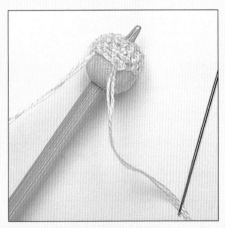

6. Increase the number of stitches at the widest part of the bead and decrease as you approach the base.

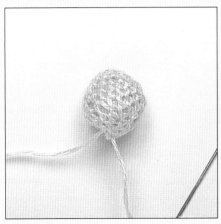

7. Remove the skewer to complete the stitching at the base.

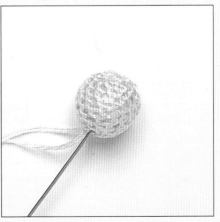

8. Thread tail and working thread into needle and take through the hole in the base to the top, leaving at least 10cm (4") of each thread.

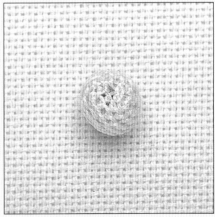

9. Attaching the grape. Thread both tails into the needle and attach the grape securely at the marked position.

ITALIAN INSERTION STITCH

This decorative stitch is used to join the side seams of the bag.

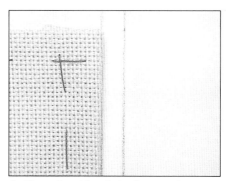

1. Place the side of the bag against one drawn line on the spacer so that the other drawn line is visible.

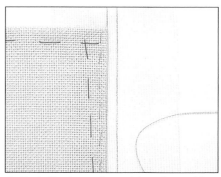

2. Tack firmly until reaching the tacking line representing the base.

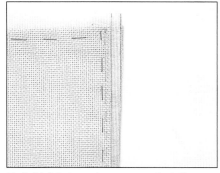

3. Fold fabric and spacer so that the top edges are even. Tack the remaining side to the second line on the spacer interfacing.

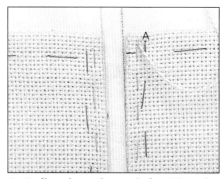

4. Italian insertion stitch. Bring the needle up at A, two threads in from the edge and two down from the top.

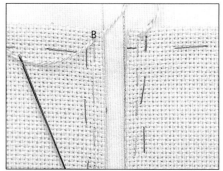

5. Take the needle from the back at B, two threads in from the edge and two down from the top.

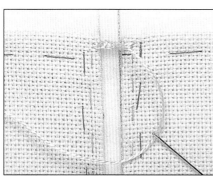

6. Repeat, working into the same holes. Work four detached blanket stitches from left to right across the loop.

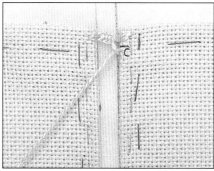

7. Work a blanket stitch on the right edge at C, two threads in from the edge and two threads down from the starting point.

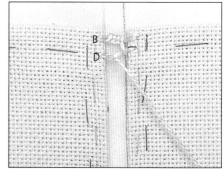

8. Work another blanket stitch on the left at D, four threads below B.

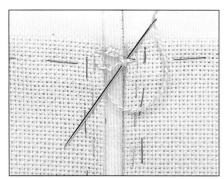

9. Work a detached blanket stitch around the centre of the blanket stitch on the right fabric edge.

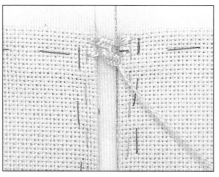

10. Work three more stitches around the same stitch, working from left to right.

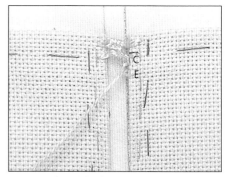

11. Work a blanket stitch on the right side at E, four threads below C.

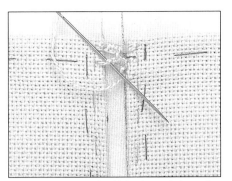

12. Work a detached blanket stitch at the centre of the stitch on the left hand side.

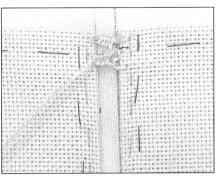

13. Work three more stitches around the same stitch, working from right to left.

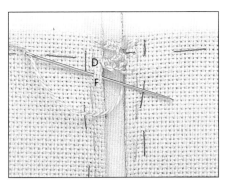

14. Work a blanket stitch on the left edge at F, four threads below D.

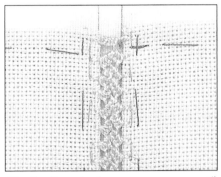

15. Continue in the same manner until reaching the base of the bag.

RAISED STEM STITCH BRANCH

The raised stem stitch is worked over a layer of padding formed with ten 22cm (8 1/2") lengths of D. Fold the bundle in half to make twenty thicknesses.

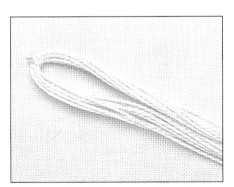

1. Secure the folded end of the threads to the top left hand end of the marked line.

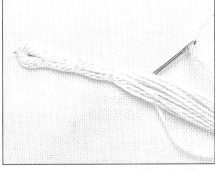

2. Using A, couch the padding in place. Bring the needle up on the marked line, take it over the padding and then back through the same hole.

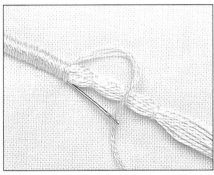

3. Using the milliner's needle, work satin stitch over the padding, angling the needle under the padding.

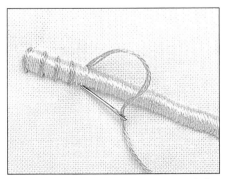

4. Create a base for the stem stitch by working a series of loose straight stitch bars at 2mm (1/16") intervals.

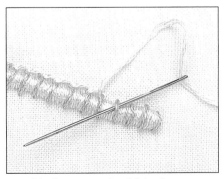

5. With three strands of B in the tapestry needle, work stem stitch into the bars, beginning at the lower right hand end.

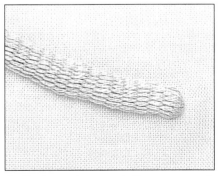

6. Begin each row at the same end, packing the rows firmly together.

CHERISH

by Alla Akselrod

This magical lace edged bag, decorated with a lily of the valley, can be filled with sweets, soap or something more precious as a lovely way of saying thank you to a special friend. The bag is made using two layers of fine cotton voile edged with cream cotton lace.

REQUIREMENTS

Fabric & Lace

35cm x 40cm wide (13 3/4" x 15 3/4") piece of cream cotton voile

60cm x 2cm wide (24" x 3/4") cream cotton lace edging

76cm x 12mm wide (30" x 1/2") cream cotton lace edging

30cm x 2cm wide (12" x 3/4") cream cotton lace beading

Threads & Needle

See page 79.

Supplies

76cm x 10mm wide (30" x 3/8") cream satin ribbon

10cm (4") embroidery hoop

Sharp lead pencil

Tracing paper

PREPARATION FOR EMBROIDERY

See the liftout sheet for the pattern and the embroidery design.
See page 118 for the cutting layout.

Transferring the design

Place a piece of tracing paper over the bag pattern. Using a black pen, trace the cutting lines for the front and the embroidery design.

With the right side of the fabric facing, place the fabric over the tracing. Pin in place to prevent movement. Using the lead pencil, trace the cutting lines and the embroidery design. Cut out the front and place in the hoop.

EMBROIDERY

See the page 79 for the step-by-step instructions for shadow work.

Order of work

Using the green thread, embroider the leaves in shadow work.

Work the two long flower stems next, followed by the two shorter ones.

Change to the ecru thread and embroider the flowers. Each large flower is stitched in padded satin stitch, while the flowers at the ends of the stems are worked with a granitos of 10 - 12 stitches. Attach each flower to the stem with a tiny straight stitch.

Single or pairs of seed stitches are worked under each of the flowers.

Scatter more tiny seed stitches around the design. Embroider a satin stitch ribbon around the stems and add two straight stitches on each side.

CONSTRUCTION

See pages 118 - 119.

THIS DESIGN USES

Granitos
Padded satin stitch
Seed stitch
Shadow work
Stem stitch
Straight stitch

———

The finished bag measures
18.5cm x 16cm wide
(7 1/4" x 6 1/4")

A gift of five sugared almonds represents health, wealth, long life, fertility and happiness. This wedding tradition dates back to the early days of European history.

SHADOW WORK

Shadow work creates a delicate effect of shading on fine fabrics. It can be worked from either side of the fabric. Here it is worked from the right side.

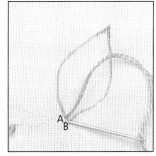

1. Begin with a waste knot. Bring needle to front at A, 1.5mm (1/16") from tip of shape. Pull through. Take needle to back at B, at tip.

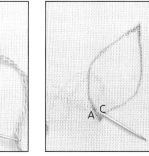

2. Pull the thread through. Re-emerge at C, on the opposite side to A.

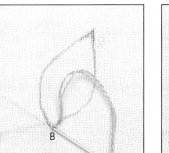

3. Pull the thread through. Take the needle to the back at B, using the same hole in the fabric as before.

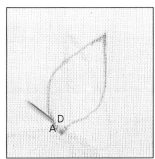

4. Pull the thread through. Re-emerge at D, 1.5mm (1/16") away from A.

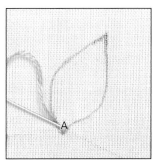

5. Pull the thread through. Take the needle to the back at A, using exactly the same hole in the fabric as before.

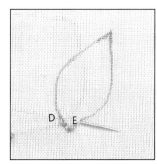

6. Pull the thread through and re-emerge at E, on the opposite side to D.

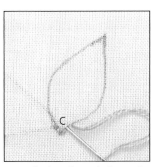

7. Pull the thread through. Take the needle to the back at C using the same hole in the fabric.

8. Continue working stitches following steps 4 - 7.

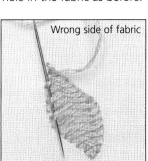

9. Continue until shape is filled. For last stitch, take needle to back and weave thread under stitches as close as possible to edge.

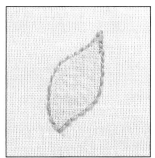

10. Right side of fabric. **Completed shadow work.**

GIDGET

by Julie Graue

Fresh lime, orange and hot pink make a dazzling combination in this gorgeous bag.

This hot pink bag is lined with gingham and features embroidered appliqué hearts and a gingham frill.

REQUIREMENTS

Fabric

30cm x 35cm wide (11 3/4" x 13 3/4") piece of pink poplin

25cm x 90cm wide (10" x 35 1/2") piece of lime Pima cotton gingham

Supplies

30cm (12") square piece of lightweight woven fusible interfacing

8cm x 20cm wide (3" x 8") piece of appliqué paper eg. *Vliesofix*

1 small clear snap fastener

Threads, Beads and Needles

DMC stranded cotton

A = 470 lt avocado green

B = 602 med cranberry

C = 3340 med apricot

Gütermann seed beads

D = 8535 green

Needles

No. 3 milliner's

THIS DESIGN USES

Beading · Bullion loop
Couching · Spider web flower

PREPARATION FOR EMBROIDERY

See the liftout sheet for the heart templates. See page 119 for the cutting layout.

Fuse the interfacing onto the wrong side of the pink poplin bag rectangle. Trace two large and two small hearts onto the appliqué paper, leaving a space around each one *(diag 1)*.

Diag 1

Cut out, leaving a border of paper around each one. Fuse the two large hearts onto the gingham and the two small hearts onto the pink poplin.

Fold the pink rectangle in half across the width and tack the foldline *(diag 2)*.

Fuse a large heart at the centre of each half of the rectangle. Centre a small heart over the large heart and fuse in place *(diag 3)*.

Diag 2

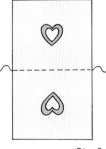

Diag 3

EMBROIDERY

See page 82 for the step-by-step instructions for spider web flower.

The flowers at the base of the handles are embroidered after the bag is constructed. Work blanket stitch in matching thread around the outside of each heart.

Embroider an apricot spider web flower and leaves in the centre of each heart.

After the bag is constructed, embroider a cranberry flower and leaves at the base of each handle, working through the frill.

CONSTRUCTION

See page 82 for instructions for making the bag.

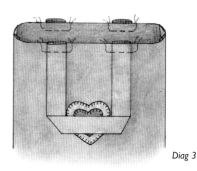

Diag 3

Fold a 1cm (³/8") hem to the inside on the outer bag and press (diag 4).

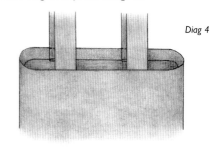

Diag 4

Fold a 1cm (³/8") hem to the outside on the lining and press. Push the lining inside the bag. Matching folded edges, pin and stitch the bag and lining together around the top (diag 5).

Diag 5

Frill

Stitch the strip into a circle. Trim and neaten the seam. Make a small double hem along each side of the frill. Stitch two rows of machine gathering, one either side of the centre of the frill. Pull up the gathers to fit the top of the bag. Pin and stitch in place with one side of the frill even with the top edge of the bag. Remove the gathering rows (diag 6).

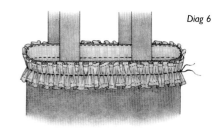

Diag 6

With right sides together, fold the pink rectangle in half and stitch the side seams (diag 1).

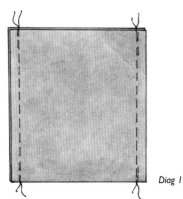

Diag 1

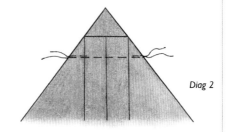

Diag 2

Press the seams open.

Fold the corners and stitch 1.5cm (⁵/8") from the corner (diag 2).

Repeat for the lining. Fold the outer bag to the right side. Leave the lining inside out.

Handles

Fuse the interfacing to the wrong side of each handle strip. With right sides together and matching raw edges, pin and stitch each strip along the long raw edges.

Turn to the right side and press. Stitch each end of the handle to the top edge of the bag 4.5cm (1 ³/4") from the side seam (diag 3).

S P I D E R   W E B   F L O W E R

These bold and colourful flowers are quick to work and have an almost three dimensional appearance. Keep the weaving tension loose when working the outer part of the flower to ensure a plump, full bloom.

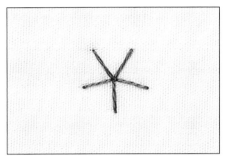

1. Work five 5mm (³/₁₆") straight stitch spokes to form the foundation of the flower.

2. Bring the thread to the front as close to the centre as possible.

3. Using the eye of the needle, weave the thread over and under the spokes until one round is complete.

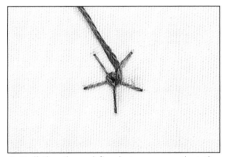

4. Pull the thread firmly to ensure that the centre is covered.

5. Continue weaving with a slightly loose tension until the spokes are covered. Take the thread to the back and finish off.

6. Work a bullion loop with 25 wraps on each side of the flower.

7. Couch each loop down with a single strand of thread.

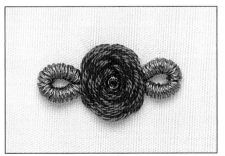

8. Stitch a seed bead at the centre of the flower.

WHAT IS PIMA COTTON?

Pima is one of the varieties of extra-long staple (ELS) cotton that is commercially grown in the USA and other parts of the world. ELS cotton is valued for its superior strength, lustre and silkiness and fabrics manufactured from this fibre are high quality.

There are five major types of ELS cotton currently grown - Egyptian, Sea Island, Pima, Asiatic and Upland.

Pima cotton was developed in the USA in the early 1900s and takes its name from the Pima indians who helped to raise the cotton in Arizona.

PERFUMED MEMORIES

by Kris Richards

The lingering fragrance of lavender is captured in this exquisite lingerie bag. Embellished with bullion roses above the silk organza pocket, it is finished with a luxurious bow, far too gorgeous to keep hidden away from view in a drawer.

THIS DESIGN USES

Bullion knot · Detached chain
French knot · Stem stitch
Straight stitch

REQUIREMENTS

Fabric

65cm x 138cm wide (25 1/2" x 54") pale pink silk dupion

14cm x 37.5cm (5 1/2" x 14 3/4") piece of ivory silk organza

Threads & Needles

See page 87.

Supplies

Fine tipped water-soluble fabric marker

Dried lavender

PREPARATION FOR EMBROIDERY

See the liftout sheet for the embroidery design and lattice template.

Transferring the design

Cut out the silk dupion front of the bag and tab following the instructions on page 119.

Place the rectangle of silk organza over the lattice pattern piece in the liftout, aligning the lower edge and sides of the organza with the lower edge and sides of the pattern piece. With the water-soluble fabric marker, trace the lattice and scallops onto the organza. Cut around the scallops.

Aligning the lower edge of the organza with the lower edge of the silk dupion, pin the two layers of fabric together. Using a narrow machine zigzag, stitch along the scallops. The embroidery will cover the stitching on the scallops. The two pieces will now be treated as the bag front.

Place the front over the embroidery design, aligning the lower edge and sides of the fabric with the lower edge and sides of the embroidery design. Mark the centre of each rose with a dot and each leaf with a fine line.

EMBROIDERY

The milliner's needle is used for the bullion roses and leaves and the crewel needle for all other embroidery.

Order of work

The bullion roses are embroidered first, then the rosebuds. Next work the leaves, daisies and French knots.

Roses

Embroider the centre petals first, then the inner and outer petals.

To give each rose a softer, more realistic look, work most of the outer petals around the lower edge and sides of the rose.

Rosebuds

Work a single rosebud at the top of each scallop peak, stitching the centre and then the outer petals.

Leaves

Work the bullion leaves among the roses, using a long anchoring stitch at the tip to give the leaves a more elegant shape.

Embroider the remaining leaves with detached chains, using the closeup photograph as a guide for placement.

Daisy petals

Fill in the remaining spaces around the roses with detached chain petals. Work two groups of three petals, one on each side of most of the roses and buds.

French knot buds

Scatter French knot buds around the roses between the leaves and daisy petals.

Lattice

Work the lattice in stem stitch.

Rose on tab

Before constructing the tab for the back of the bag, embroider the rose, leaves, daisy petals and French knot buds in the same manner as the embroidery on the scallops.

CONSTRUCTION

See pages 119 - 120.

THREADS AND NEEDLES

Anchor stranded cotton

A = 892 ultra lt shell pink

DMC stranded cotton

B = 316 med antique mauve

C = 640 vy dk beige-grey

D = 778 vy lt antique mauve

E = 3012 med khaki green

F = 3042 lt antique violet

G = 3726 dk antique mauve

H = 3740 dk antique violet

Needles

No. 7 milliner's

No. 9 crewel

EMBROIDERY KEY

All embroidery is worked with two strands unless otherwise specified.

Large roses

Centre = G
(2 bullion knots, 6 wraps)

Inner petals = B
(3 bullion knots, 12 wraps)

Outer petals = D (5 bullion knots, 12 wraps)

Medium roses

Centre = G
(2 bullion knots, 6 wraps)

Inner petals = B
(3 bullion knots, 12 wraps)

Outer petals = D (4 bullion knots, 12 wraps)

Small roses

Centre = G
(2 bullion knots, 6 wraps)

Inner petals = B
(3 bullion knots, 12 wraps)

Outer petals = D
(3 bullion knots, 12 wraps)

Rosebuds

Centre = G
(2 bullion knots, 6 wraps)

Outer petals = B
(2 bullion knots, 12 wraps)

Leaves = E
(1 strand, 2 bullion knots
10 - 15 wraps, straight stitch)
or C (1 strand, detached chain)

Daisy petals = F
(1 strand, detached chain)

French knot buds = H
(French knot, 2 wraps)

Lattice = A (1 strand, stem stitch)

THE COLOURS KRIS HAS CHOSEN FOR HER BULLION ROSES BEAUTIFULLY COMPLEMENT THE
DUPION SILK. A LAVENDER SCENTED LINGERIE BAG IS A PERFECT GIFT FOR THE BRIDE-TO-BE.

MIDNIGHT FANTASY

by Julie Graue

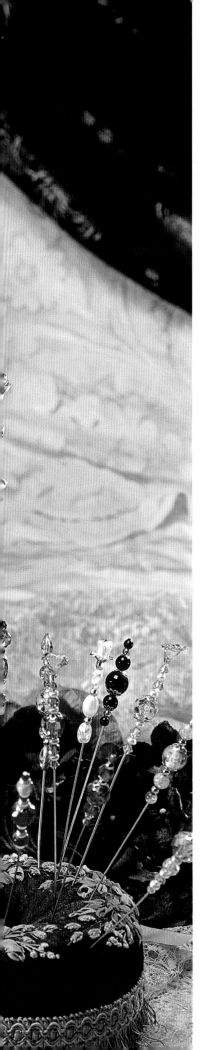

On a background of opulent black quilted satin, Julie has cleverly backsmocked luxurious fuchsia shantung to create a band of subtle texture at the front of the bag. A fantastic combination of beautiful braid, ribbon, piping and a fringe of beads add further interest.

REQUIREMENTS

Fabric

50cm x 112cm wide (20" x 44") piece of black quilted satin

45cm x 150cm wide (17 3/4" x 59") piece of fuchsia satin-backed shantung

Supplies

40cm x 112cm wide (16" x 44") piece of black heavyweight fusible interfacing

60cm (23 1/2") black satin mini piping

35cm (13 3/4") rose pink fringe beading

Mokuba frill ribbon no. 4571
1.85m (2yd) no. 17 green

Mokuba braid no. 9314
85cm (33 1/2") no. 8 lavender

14cm x 26cm wide (5 1/2" x 10 1/4") piece of template plastic

Chalk based fabric marker

No. 8 crewel needle

Thread

Madeira stranded silk
0703 fuchsia

CUTTING OUT

See page 120 for the cutting layouts.

Fuchsia satin backed shantung

Front insert: cut one,
8cm x 122cm wide (3 1/4" x 48")

Trace the pattern pieces onto lightweight interfacing or tracing paper, transferring the pattern markings. Cut out the remaining pieces following the instructions on page 120.

PREPARATION AND PLEATING

To prevent fraying, neaten the upper and lower raw edges with a machine zigzag or overlock stitch.

Pleat 7 full space rows (including two holding rows) with the top holding row 1cm (3/8") from the upper raw edge.

Unpick the pleating threads for 1cm (3/8") at each side and tie off to measure 28cm (11").

SMOCKING

Backsmocking

Row 1. Beginning at the left hand side of the first pleat on row 1, work stem stitch across the row using 2 strands of silk.

Row 5. Repeat row 1.

CONSTRUCTION

See page 90 for step-by-step instructions for making the bag. See pages 120 - 121 for making and attaching the lining and handles.

CONSTRUCTING
THE BAG

★

1. Piping the smocked insert

Cut two pieces of piping to fit the long edges of the smocked insert. Pin and tack one piece of piping to the right side of the insert aligning the corded edge of the piping with the upper backsmocked row, using the pleating threads as a guide. Stitch along the piping stitchline *(diag 1)*. Repeat for the lower edge of the band.

Diag 1

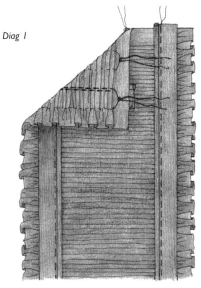

2. Attaching front side panels

Fuse interfacing to the wrong side of both front side panel pieces. With right sides together and matching raw edges, pin one front side panel to one piped edge of the insert. Stitch in between the piping and the previous row of stitching *(diag 2)*. Trim and neaten the seam. Repeat for the remaining front side panel.

Diag 2

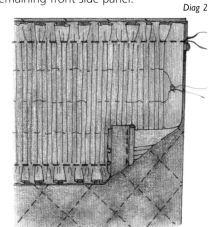

WORKING
STEM STITCH

1. Ensure that you keep a firm, even tension.

2. After working only a few stitches the row may appear to slope. It is not crooked, the fabric is skewing. As you continue stitching the row will appear straight.

3. Keep the needle horizontal for each stitch.

4. Every so often, let the needle and thread dangle to untwist the thread.

3. Attaching frill ribbon

Cut two pieces of green frilled ribbon to fit the piped edges of the insert. Position the straight edge of one piece of ribbon along one piped edge of the panel.

Pin and stitch in place as close to the edge of the ribbon as possible. Stitch again, close to the frilled edge of the ribbon (diag 3). Attach the remaining ribbon to the other side of the panel in the same manner.

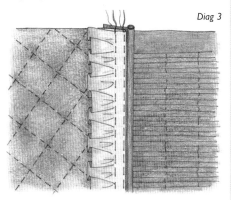

Diag 3

4. Attaching the top panels to the front and back

Fuse interfacing to the wrong side of both top quilted panel pieces and the quilted back piece. With right sides together and matching raw edges, pin one top panel to the bag front. Stitch (diag 4). Trim and neaten the seam. Press towards the top panel. Repeat for the back.

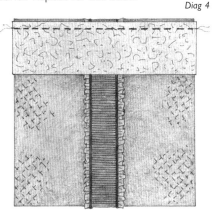

Diag 4

5. Attaching the beaded fringe

Positioning the lower edge of the beading heading along the seam line joining the top panel to the bag front. Remove one drop of beads at each side ensuring the beading thread is secure. Pin and stitch along the top edge of the heading, taking care to keep the beads out of the way (diag 5).

Diag 5

6. Side seams

With right sides together and matching raw edges and top panel seam lines, pin the front to the back at the sides. Stitch, again taking care to avoid any beads (diag 6). Press the seam open.

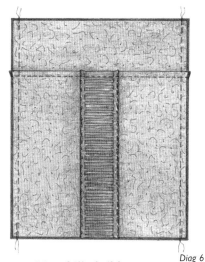

Diag 6

7. Attaching frilled ribbon to beading heading

Aligning the frilled seam of the ribbon with the upper edge of the beading heading and with the frilled edge facing towards the beading, pin the ribbon around the entire bag, beginning at one side seam. On the back, the frilled edge of the ribbon will just touch the top panel seamline. Turn under the end of the ribbon 5mm (1/4") and overlap slightly at the start (diag 7).

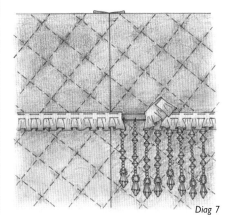

Diag 7

Stitch first, close to the straight edge of the ribbon. Using a zipper foot, stitch a second row along the stitchline on the ribbon frill.

8. Attaching the base

Fuse interfacing to the wrong side of the quilted base piece. Turn the bag to the inside. With right sides together and matching raw edges and side seams to the placement marks on the pattern, pin the base to the bag. Stitch (diag 8).

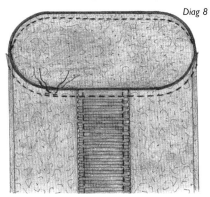

Diag 8

Clip the curves in the seam allowance where necessary. Press gently. Remove the pleating threads from the smocking.

9. Securing template plastic

Place the plastic base into the base of the bag so that it sits within the seam allowance. Using a double sewing thread, lace the plastic in position by stitching from side to side several times through the seam allowance (diag 9).

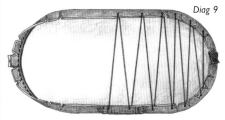

Diag 9

BIRD OF PARADISE

The slightly coarse fibre
of black linen provides a
wonderful contrast to the rich
embroidery on the front of
the majestic shoulder bag.

Jenny Crowe borrows from
ancient tradition
to create this indispensible item
for civilised beings.

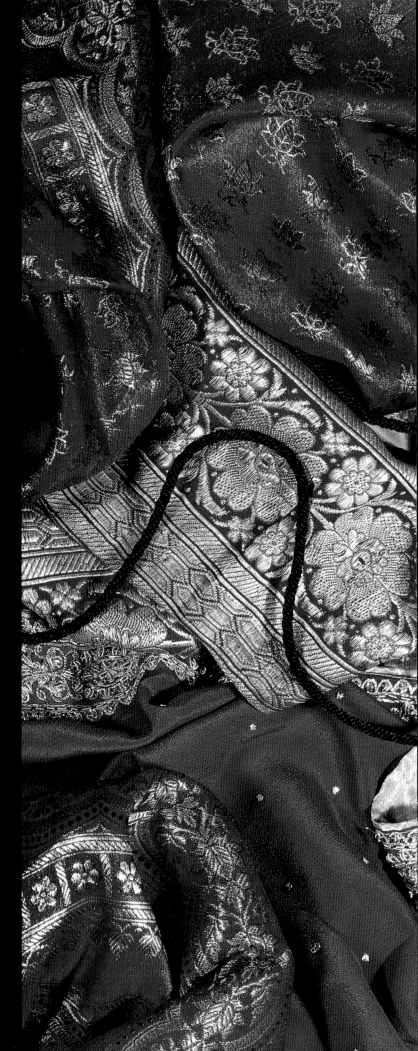

The lined bag is lavishly embroidered on the front flap and a smaller motif is stitched on the back. A black twisted rayon cord forms the shoulder strap. The flap is secured with a Chinese ball button and a tasselled loop.

REQUIREMENTS

Fabric

45cm x 65cm wide (17 3/4" x 25 5/8") piece of black linen

35cm x 50cm wide (13 3/4" x 19 5/8") piece of black polyester lining

Supplies

1.4m x 4mm wide (1yd 19" x 3/16") black rayon cord

1 x 5cm (2") long black tassel with a 2cm (3/4") loop

1 x 12mm (1/2") black Chinese ball button

19cm x 12mm wide (7 1/2" x 1/2") black non-roll elastic

25cm x 35cm wide (9 3/4" x 13 3/4") piece of thin fusible wadding eg Pellon

20cm (8") embroidery hoop

Tracing paper

Chalk-based fabric marker

Threads & Needles

See page 96.

PREPARATION FOR EMBROIDERY

See the liftout sheet for the pattern and embroidery designs.

Cut a 41cm x 30.5cm wide (16" x 12") rectangle for the flap and back of the bag. This will be cut to its exact shape after the embroidery is complete.

Trace the pattern pieces onto the tracing paper.

Cut out all pieces following the instructions and cutting layouts on page 112. Transfer the pattern markings.

Transferring the designs

Trace the pattern piece for the flap and back of the bag, including the embroidery designs, onto tracing paper.

The embroidery on the flap is completed before transferring the embroidery design to the back of the bag.

Centre the tracing onto the right side of the rectangle of black linen. Ensure the grain of the fabric is aligned with the marked grainline on the pattern piece. Pin in place to prevent movement.

Using a large needle, pierce holes in the tracing along the lines of the front design and at the positions of the flowers on the flap. Dot each hole with the chalk-based fabric marker. Remove the tracing.

Join the dots along the design lines so you have unbroken guidelines for working the embroidery. This will make it easier to achieve evenly shaped curves and straight lines when stitching.

After the embroidery on the flap is complete, reposition the tracing over the fabric and transfer the back motif in the same manner as the front design.

EMBROIDERY

Columns of dusky mauve flowers alternated with soft grey stripes fan out from a scalloped semi-circle on the front flap of the bag. Larger densely embroidered scallops border the flap.

The back of the bag is embroidered with a circular motif similar to the central semi-circle on the front.

Use the milliner's needle for working the bullion knots and the crewel needle for all other embroidery.

Outer section of front flap

Begin at the outer edge of the flap and stitch three parallel rows of chain stitch in black thread.

Stitch the first and third rows and then work the middle row to ensure your rows fill the required space.

Outline the outer scallops with two rows of chain stitch and then two rows of stem stitch. Fill the middle of each scallop with satin stitch.

Between each scallop, stitch two French knots near the black border.

Work the flowers above the French knots next. Stitch two detached chains, one inside the other, for the stems. Work the leaves in the same manner. Add a straight stitch to either side of each leaf using the metallic thread. For each flower, embroider five straight stitches. Begin at the same point at the base of the flower and fan them out.

Using the same thread, stitch a detached chain on either side of the centre straight stitch. Stitch three French knots in a triangle around each flower.

Middle section of front flap

Stitch the stripes next. Work a line of chain stitch for the centre of each stripe and then border this with lines of stem stitch.

Columns of mauve flowers are alternated with the stripes. Begin at the base of a column with a large mauve flower consisting of five bullion knots.

Work three medium flowers up the column. Work three bullion knots for each flower and gradually decrease the number of wraps used as you work up the column.

Using the lighter mauve thread, stitch a small flower with two bullion knots. Above this, stitch three French knot buds, gradually decreasing their size as you work towards the centre. Using F, add two detached chain leaves to the three lower flowers in each column. Add two detached chain leaves to the remaining flowers using K.

Inner section of front flap

Outline the semi-circle at the centre with chain stitch. Embroider six rows of stem stitch closely together just beyond the line of chain stitch. Use the metallic thread for the sixth row.

Fill the semi-circle with satin stitch, just covering the inside half of the chain stitch outline.

Using the darker mauve thread, outline the scallops in chain stitch. Embroider a second row of chain stitch with the lighter olive green thread. Fill in each scallop with satin stitch.

Finally, add French knots to the outer edge of the motif. Stitch green French knots at the peaks and golden olive knots at the centre of each curve. Between these knots, embroider French knots with the metallic thread.

Back motif

Stitch the back motif in a similar manner to the inner scalloped motif on the front flap. However, at the very centre, embroider a blanket stitch pinwheel rather than a satin stitched centre. Work the French knots around the outer edge using only the stranded cotton threads.

CONSTRUCTION

See pages 121-123.

THREADS & NEEDLES

DMC stranded cotton

A = 310 black

B = 645 vy dk beaver grey

C = 646 dk beaver grey

D = 832 golden olive

E = 844 ultra dk beaver grey

F = 934 black avocado green

G = 3041 med antique mauve

H = 3042 lt antique mauve

I = 3072 vy lt beaver grey

J = 3753 ultra vy lt antique blue

Anchor stranded cotton

K = 846 dk olive green

L = 856 med olive green

Madeira stranded metallic thread

M = 5014 black-gold

Needles

No. 8 crewel

No. 9 milliner's

EMBROIDERY KEY

All embroidery is worked with two strands of thread unless otherwise specified.

Outer section of front flap

Outer border = A (3 strands, chain stitch)

Outer scallops

Scallops = B (chain stitch), I (stem stitch)
J (3 strands, satin stitch)

Knots between scallops = F
(3 strands, French knot, 3 wraps)

Flowers between outer scallops

Stem = I (detached chain)

Leaves = K (detached chain)
M (straight stitch)

Flower = G (straight stitch detached chain)

Buds = D (French knot, 2 wraps)

Middle section of front flap

Stripes

Inner stripe = E (chain stitch)

Outer stripes = C (stem stitch)

Large mauve flowers

Petals = G
(5 bullion knots, 8 wraps)

Leaves = F (detached chain)

Medium mauve flowers

Petals = G
(3 bullion knots
4 - 6 wraps)

Leaves = F or K (detached chain)

Small mauve flowers

Petals = H
(2 bullion knots, 3 wraps)

Leaves = K (detached chain)

Buds = H (French knot, 1 - 2 wraps)

Inner scalloped motif

Centre = K (satin stitch)
K (3 strands, chain stitch)
B (stem stitch), M (stem stitch)
K (3 strands, chain stitch)
B (stem stitch), M (stem stitch)

Scallops = G (chain stitch), H (satin stitch)

Outer edge = L (chain stitch), D, K
and M (French knot, 2 wraps)

Back motif

Centre = K (blanket stitch)
B (stem stitch), M (stem stitch)

Scallops = G (chain stitch), H (satin stitch)

Outer edge = L (chain stitch)
D and K (French knot, 2 wraps)

HINTS ON COLOUR

1. Study your environment as nature provides many examples of wonderful colour schemes.

2. When purchasing threads, always place your selection on a piece of the fabric you will be stitching on.

Different coloured grounds can alter the appearance of the thread colours.

3. Colours change depending on the strength and type of light they are viewed in.

If possible, select your colours in light similar to that in the final surroundings for the project.

THIS DESIGN USES

Blanket stitch · Bullion knot
Chain stitch · Detached chain
French knot · Satin stitch
Stem stitch · Straight stitch

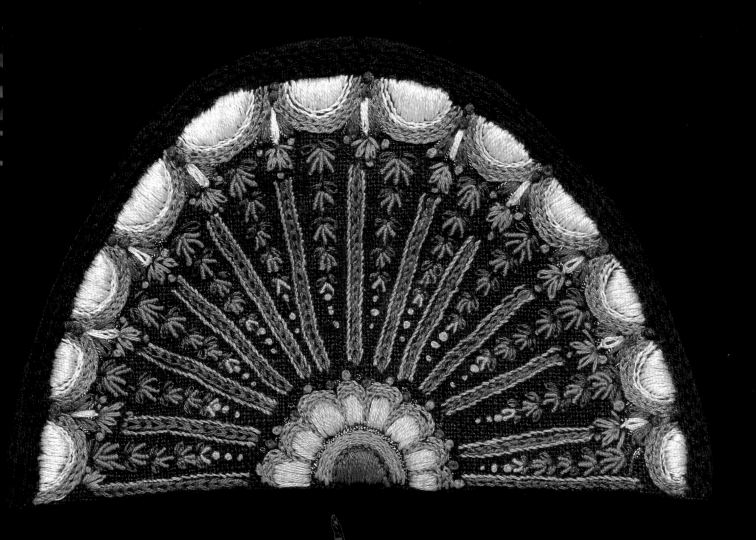

BIRD OF
PARADISE

The finished shoulder bag

measures 17.5cm x 18cm wide

(6 $\frac{7}{8}$" x 7 $\frac{1}{8}$").

BONNIE WEE BAG

by Judy Stephenson

The rich colours of the Scottish thistle burst forth proudly on this beautiful little bag

Judy has used Casalguidi techniques, such as four sided stitch, padding and detached blanket stitch, to create a richly textured surface. The twisted cord drawstring is held by needle-woven bars placed over a foundation of four sided stitch. The bag is lined with a rich plum satin.

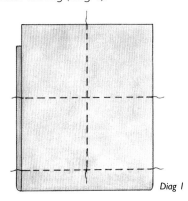

REQUIREMENTS

Fabric

46cm x 22cm wide (18" x 8 3/4") piece of 25 count cream Lugana

45cm x 22cm wide (17 3/4" x 8 3/4") piece of plum satin

Supplies

10cm x 5cm wide (4" x 2") piece of green felt

Contrasting machine sewing thread

Tracing paper

Sharp lead pencil

Small amount of fibre-fill

15cm (6") embroidery hoop

Threads & Needles

See page 102.

PREPARATION FOR EMBROIDERY

See the liftout sheet for the embroidery design and thistle templates.

Preparing the fabric

Neaten all edges of the fabric with a machine zigzag or overlock stitch. Turn each short end under 1.5cm (5/8") of the fabric and tack.

Fold the fabric in half and work a row of tacking along the foldline with the machine sewing thread. This line represents the lower edge of the bag.

Divide the front into quarters by working a line of horizontal, then vertical tacking *(diag 1)*.

Diag 1

The lines of tacking remain in place until all embroidery is complete.

Transferring the design

Using a black pen, trace the design onto the tracing paper. Tape the tracing to a window or light box.

With right side up, place the prepared fabric over the tracing, aligning the tacking lines with the placement marks. Tape in place. The light shining through will make the design easy to see. Using the pencil, trace the design.

THIS DESIGN USES

Chain stitch

Detached blanket stitch

Four sided stitch

Needleweaving

Stem stitch

Straight stitch

EMBROIDERY

See page 101 for step-by-step instructions for four sided stitch and page 103 for working the thistle.

The thistle embroidery is worked in the hoop.

Use the crewel needle for the leaves and thorns and the tapestry needle for all other embroidery.

Order of work

Drawstring foundation

Three rows of four sided stitch form the foundation for the loops and twisted cord drawstring.

Count seventeen threads down from the folded edge. Begin the first stitch at the centre tacking line.

Work sixteen stitches on each side of the central tacking line. Work a further two rows directly below. The holes of the centre row are shared by the adjacent rows.

Embroider a panel of four sided stitch, in the same position, on the back of the bag.

Loops

Bring the needle to the front at A, the central hole of the top row of four sided stitch. Take it to the back through the corresponding hole B, on the lower row of four sided stitch (diag 2).

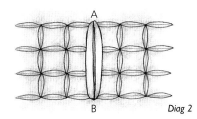

Diag 2

Repeat. Bring the needle to the front at A again and weave under and over the two straight stitches. Weave until reaching B (diag 3).

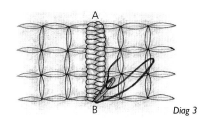

Diag 3

Take the needle to the back through the lower hole at B and secure the thread at the back.

Make the two end loops in the same manner, using the first holes in from the end of the row.

Repeat on the back of the bag.

Thistle

Stem

Using three strands of F, work two rows of chain stitch to form the stem. With one strand of G, embroider straight stitches for the thorns.

Leaves

Stitch the long centre veins with G. Using F, stem stitch around the outline of the central section of each leaf. Fill in the remainder of this section with rows of stem stitch. Work the smaller sections in the same manner. Using G add straight stitches for the thorns at the tips of each leaf. Remove the fabric from the hoop.

Complete the thistle head following the step-by-step instructions.

Cord and tassels

See page 123.

CONSTRUCTION

See page 123.

FOUR SIDED STITCH

Also known as square open work stitch and four sided open work stitch. This stitch is worked from right to left.

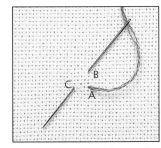

1. Bring the needle to the front at A. Take to the back at B, four threads above A. Emerge at C, four threads below and four to the left.

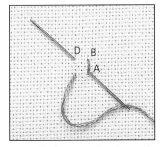

2. Pull the needle through and insert at A. Bring to the front at D, four threads above and four to the left.

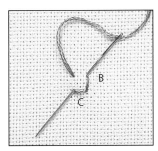

3. Insert the needle at B and re-emerge at C.

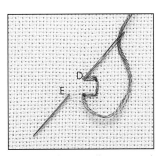

4. Insert the needle at D and emerge at E, four threads below and four to the left.

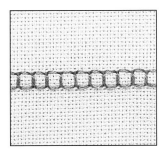

5. Continue in this manner to the end of the row. **Completed four sided stitch.**

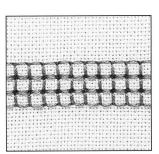

6. When working adjacent rows, use the same holes as the previous row.

THREADS & NEEDLES

Presencia stranded cotton

A = 2171 vy dk burgundy (2 skeins)

B = 2246 vy dk tea rose (2 skeins)

C = 2415 wine (2 skeins)

D = 3000 stone

E = 5140 lt fern green

F = 5151 fern green (3 skeins)

G = 8492 dk beaver grey

Needles

No. 8 crewel

No. 24 tapestry

EMBROIDERY KEY

All embroidery is worked with three strands unless otherwise specified.

Drawstring foundation

Border = D (four sided stitch)

Loops = D (6 strands
needleweaving)

Thistle

Head = A, B and C (6 strands)

Base = F (chain stitch
detached blanket stitch)
E and G (straight stitch)

Stem = F (chain stitch)

Thorns = G (straight stitch)

Leaves

Veins = G (stem stitch)

Outline and filling = F (stem stitch)

Thorns = G (1 strand
straight stitch)

Drawstring cord = F (twisted cord)

Tassel

Tuft = A, B, and C

Base = F (detached
blanket stitch)

HINTS • *When selecting tacking thread, choose a colour that will not leave a residue of dye, as this may permanently damage your work.* • *Beware of dark reds and black.*

• *Select white if it will show up, otherwise choose a pastel shade.*

THISTLE

The thistle head is created by folding lengths of thread, then working a raised base over felt padding. The lower section of the threads helps to pad the base. For the head, cut two 2m (2yd 7") lengths each of A, B and C.

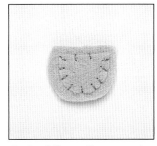

1. Padding. Cut out the two felt shapes and join together with several small stitches.

2. Place on the fabric at the marked centre point, with the smaller shape underneath. Attach the lower two thirds to the fabric.

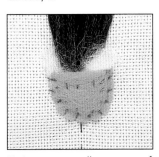

3. Thistle head. Fold A, B and C together four times. Tie together with 2 strands, 30cm (12") long, of green thread, F.

4. Thread both ends into a needle and take the needle through the opening at the upper edge of the padding.

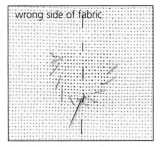

wrong side of fabric

5. Take the needle to the back at the base of the padding.

6. Pull the folded threads down under the padding to the base. Secure the thread on the back of the fabric.

7. Insert a small amount of fibre-fill on each side of the folded threads to ensure a rounded appearance.

8. Using one strand of F, secure upper edge of base to fabric by stitching through folded threads and felt to back of fabric.

9. Thistle base. Using three strands of F, work loose chain stitch across the upper edge of the felt.

10. Bring needle to front at the left hand side and work a row of detached blanket stitch. Do not stitch through the felt.

11. Take needle to the back just beside the felt and emerge at left hand side. Work a second row of detached blanket stitch.

12. Continue in this manner until the base is covered, ensuring that the base maintains its shape.

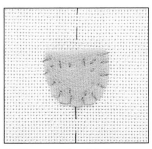

13. Trim the thistle head and comb to shape. **Completed thistle.**

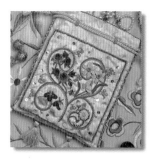

Elizabethan Sweetbag

*For colour photos and full details,
see pages 6 - 17.*

CUTTING OUT

Strawberry silk dupion

Cut in half to measure 19cm x 16cm wide (7 1/2" x 6 1/4").

CUTTING LAYOUTS

Gold silk damask
1. Front

Strawberry silk dupion
1. Front and back lining

CONSTRUCTION

For step-by-step construction see page 13.

Twisted cord

Cut a 1.9m (2yd 3") length each of C, F, H and J. Loop F through J *(diag 1)*.

Diag 1

Make a twisted cord. Loop C through H, slide the looped end of the first cord to the point where the two colours are looped through one another before beginning to twist the second cord *(diag 2)*.

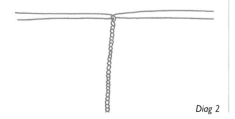

Diag 2

Twist up the second cord. Twist the two cords into one. Knot each end, leaving a 2.5cm (1") tail. Cut and tease out the strands of thread *(diag 3)*.

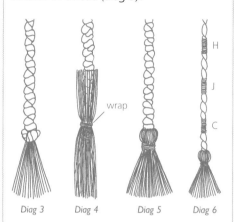

Diag 3   Diag 4   Diag 5   Diag 6

Cut ten 9cm (3 1/2") lengths of E.

Position them around the knot and wrap above the knot to hold in place *(diag 4)*.

Fold the ends down over the knot and wrap, using one strand of H *(diag 5)*. Repeat for the remaining end of the cord. Tease out the strands of thread and trim so they are even.

Wrap three separate bands of colour near each end of the cord, using a single strand each of C, H and J *(diag 6)*.

Stitch the cord in place, along the side seam ensuring that the tassels hang below the bag.

Cut the rayon cord in half and wrap each end with a single strand of J, leaving 13mm (1/2") of cord protruding. Tease out the ends of the cord and trim to neaten.

Thread each cord through the needle woven bars, knotting one on the left and one on the right.

Central tassels

Cut ten 10cm (4") lengths of E. Loop all the lengths through the blanket stitch bar and wrap tightly together with one strand of H. Trim to measure 3.5cm (1 3/8").

Work another tassel for the remaining blanket stitch bar in the same manner.

Country Life

*For colour photos and full details,
see pages 18 - 23.*

CUTTING OUT

Where a pattern piece is not provided, use the following measurements.

Linen and interfacing

Cut two rectangles, each 32cm x 35cm wide (12 1/2" x 13 3/4") for the front pocket and the back of the bag. These pieces will be cut to their exact shape after the embroidery is complete. Cut two pieces, each 68cm x 8cm wide (26 3/4" x 3 1/8") for the straps.

Linen

Cut two pieces on the bias, each 85cm x 3cm wide (33 1/2" x 1 1/4") for the piping.

Trace the remaining pattern pieces for the bag and lining onto tracing paper. Cut out following the cutting layouts.

CUTTING LAYOUTS

Linen

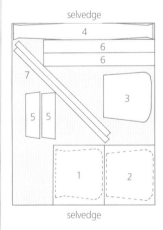

1. Pocket rectangle
2. Back rectangle
3. Front
4. Gusset
5. Front and back facings
6. Strap
7. Piping

Polyester Lining

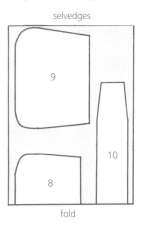

selvedges

9

10

8

fold

8. Pocket lining
9. Front and back lining
10. Gusset lining

Interfacing

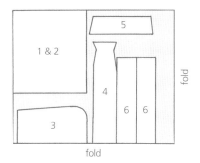

5

1 & 2

4

6 6

3

fold

fold

1. Pocket rectangle
2. Back rectangle
3. Front
4. Gusset
5. Front and back facings
6. Strap

CONSTRUCTION

All seam allowances are 1cm (3/8") unless otherwise specified. The shaded areas on the diagrams indicate the right side of the fabric.

1. Preparation

When the embroidery is complete, cut out the pieces for the front pocket and the back following the marked cutting lines. Place the embroidery face down on a well padded surface and carefully press.

Fuse the interfacings to the wrong side of all the remaining bag pieces.

2. Making the piping

Cut the piping cord in half. With the wrong side of one piece of piping fabric

facing up, place one length of cord along the centre *(diag 1)*.

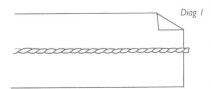

Diag 1

Fold the fabric over the cord. Pin the two layers of fabric together, keeping the cord against the fold. Stitch close to the cord so it is completely enclosed *(diag 2)*.

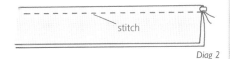

stitch

Diag 2

Cover remaining cord in the same manner.

3. Making the front pocket

With right sides together and matching raw edges, pin the upper edge of the pocket lining to the edge of the pocket facing. Stitch *(diag 3)*.

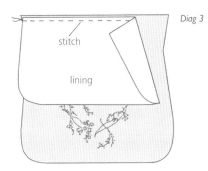

Diag 3

stitch

lining

Press the lining away from the pocket. Following the marked fold line, fold the pocket facing to the back and press.

Matching raw edges, tack the lining to the pocket around the outer edges *(diag 4)*.

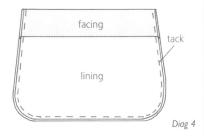

facing

tack

lining

Diag 4

4. Attaching the front pocket

Matching placement marks and with the lining facing the right side of the front,

place the pocket onto the front of the bag. Pin and tack the layers together around the outer edges *(diag 5)*.

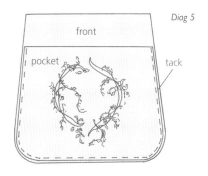

Diag 5

front

pocket

tack

5. Attaching the piping

Beginning with 1cm (3/8") curving into the seam allowance, pin one length of piping around the outer edge of the front. At the curved corner, clip the piping heading and ease the piping slightly *(diag 6)*.

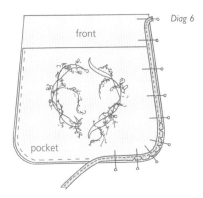

Diag 6

front

pocket

Continue pinning and clipping until reaching the opposite end. Trim any excess length of piping allowing 1cm (3/8") to curve into the seam allowance as before. Stitch the piping to the front along the piping stitch line *(diag 7)*.

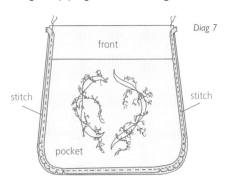

Diag 7

front

stitch

stitch

pocket

Attach the second length of piping to the back of the bag in the same manner.

6. Attaching the gusset

With the wrong side of the gusset facing up, pin the buckram onto the base at the marked position. Stitch along the short sides (diag 8).

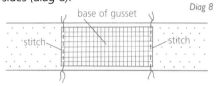

Diag 8

Referring to the pattern for placement, stitch a row of staystitching on either side of the gusset, just within the seam allowance. Clip the seam allowance at 1cm (³⁄₈") intervals along the staystitched areas (diag 9).

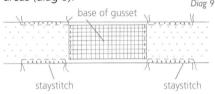

Diag 9

Place the gusset onto the front with right sides together. Beginning at the marked centre at the base and finishing at the upper edge of the bag, pin one long side of the gusset to the piped edge of the front. The fold line for the gusset facing should align 2.5cm (1") below the beginning of the piping (diag 10).

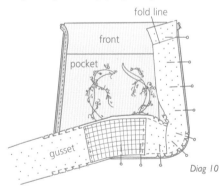

Diag 10

Tack the layers together. With the wrong side of the front uppermost, stitch just beside the piping stitch line, finishing at the gusset facing fold line (diag 11).

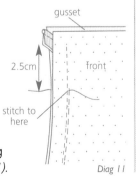

Diag 11

Beginning at the marked centre again, pin and stitch the second half of the gusset to the front in the same manner. Trim the seams and clip the curves. Press the seam allowance away from the gusset. Attach the remaining long side of the gusset to the back in the same manner. Turn the bag with the right side facing out.

7. Making the straps

With right sides together and matching raw edges, fold one strap in half lengthwise. Stitch down the long side (diag 12).

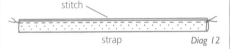

Diag 12

Turn the strap to the right side and press. Repeat for the second strap.

8. Attaching the straps

Matching raw edges, pin the ends of one strap at the marked position on the front of the bag. Securing the ends firmly, stitch in place (diag 13).

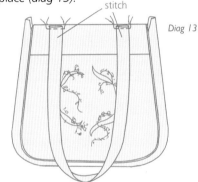

Diag 13

Attach the remaining strap to the back in the same manner.

9. Facing the top edges

With right sides together and matching raw edges, pin the facing onto the upper edge of the front. Keeping the gusset facing out of the way, stitch down the side of one front corner finishing at the fold line for the gusset facing (diag 14).

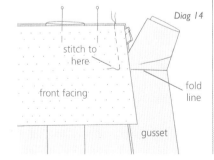

Diag 14

Stitch down the side of the remaining front corner in the same manner. Stitch across the upper edge of the front and front facing (diag 15).

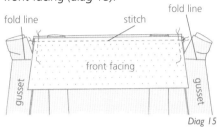

Diag 15

Trim the seams and clip the corners. Keeping the lower section of the bag out of the way and with right sides together, pin the unstitched sections of the front facing to the gusset facings. Beginning at the gusset facing fold line and stitching towards the raw edges, stitch the facings together (diag 16).

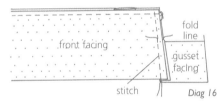

Diag 16

Press the seams away from the gusset. Attach the facing to the back of the bag in the same manner.

10. Making the lining

Leaving a 10cm (4") opening in one side at the base, join the gusset lining to the front and back linings (diag 17).

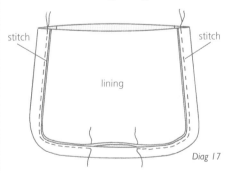

Diag 17

11. Attaching the lining

With right sides together, place the bag inside the lining. Aligning seams and matching raw edges, pin the lower edge of the facings to the upper edge of the lining. Stitch (diag 18).

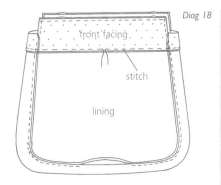

Diag 18

Turn the bag to the right side through the opening in the lining. Fold under the raw edges of the opening and stitch closed *(diag 19)*.

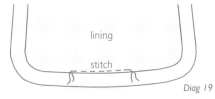

Diag 19

12. Finishing

Place the lining inside the bag. Press the facings flat. On the inside, fasten the facings to the bag by hand stitching the gusset facing seams to the seam allowances beneath. Remove any tacking threads.

Spring Bouquet

For colour photos and full details, see pages 24 - 29.

CUTTING OUT

Ivory damask

Cut a rectangle 45cm x 28cm wide (17 3/4" x 11") for the purse. Cut a rectangle 10cm x 22cm wide (4" x 8 5/8") for the zip tab. The remaining piece is for the tissue holder. These pieces will be cut to their exact shapes after the embroidery is complete.

Calico and thin wadding

Using the purse pattern, cut one piece from the calico for the purse lining and one piece from the wadding for the purse padding. Transfer all pattern markings to the calico.

Ivory moiré

Cut a rectangle, 14cm x 21cm wide (5 1/2" x 8 1/4") for the tissue holder lining. Cut two pieces, each 3cm x 11.5cm wide (1 1/4" x 4 1/2") for binding the ends of the tissue holder.

CUTTING LAYOUTS

Ivory damask

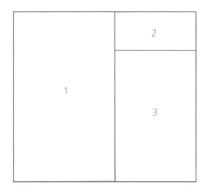

1. Purse front and back
2. Zip tab
3. Tissue holder

Ivory moiré

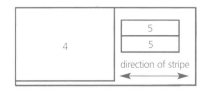

4. Tissue holder lining
5. Tissue holder binding

CONSTRUCTION

All seam allowances are 1cm (3/8") unless otherwise specified. The shaded areas on the diagrams indicate the right side of the fabric.

Cosmetic purse

1. Preparation

Place the embroidered pieces face down on a well padded surface, such as a folded flannelette sheet, and press. Cut out along the marked cutting lines.

2. Joining the padding and lining

Place the piece embroidered for the purse, face down on a flat surface. Matching raw edges, place the wadding over the damask and the calico, with the markings showing, on top of the wadding *(diag 1)*.

Pin and tack the three layers together. Treat as one layer from now on. Using a long straight stitch, machine stitch around all sides 5mm (3/16") from the raw edges. Trim and neaten the upper and lower curved edges with a zigzag or overlock stitch *(diag 2)*.

Diag 1

3. Inserting the zip

Open the zip. With right sides together, pin one side of the zip along the upper edge of the purse front. Align the metal stopper with the side seam stitch line and the edge of the zip tape with the neatened edge of the opening. The end of the zip will extend past the remaining side seam stitch line *(diag 3)*.

Diag 2

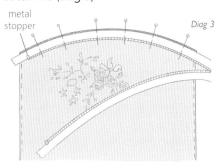

Diag 3

Tack in place. Using a zipper foot, stitch across the upper edge close to the zip teeth. Close the zip. With right sides together, fold the purse at the base. Pin and tack the remaining half of the zip to the upper edge of the purse back. Open the zip and stitch in the same manner as the front *(diag 4)*. Press.

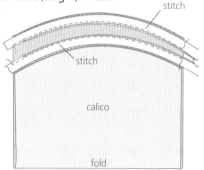

Diag 4

4. Joining the side seams

Partly close the zip. With right sides together, upper edges even and zip teeth aligned, pin and tack the side seams. Stitch the seams, stitching through the ends of the zip on both sides *(diag 5)*.

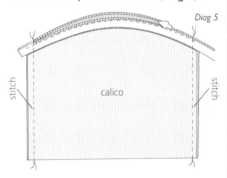

Diag 5

Trim the seam allowances to 6mm (1/4") and cut off the excess length of the zip. Reinforce the cut end of the zip by hand stitching the zip teeth together close to the stitch line *(diag 6)*.

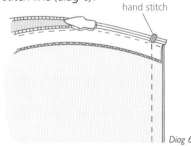

Diag 6

Cut two pieces of bias binding, each 17.5cm (6 7/8") long. With the right side of the binding facing the lining, place one length of binding along one side seam. Ensure the first pressed fold in the binding is aligned with the stitch line and 1cm (3/8") extends beyond the upper edge of the purse. Pin and tack in place *(diag 7)*.

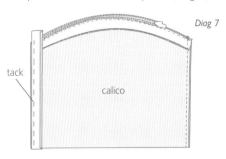

Diag 7

Stitch the binding to the purse along the previous stitch line. Fold in the raw end of the binding level with the upper edge of the purse. Fold the binding around the seam allowance. Pin and tack in place. Using matching thread, hand stitch the second fold of the binding to the previous stitch line *(diag 8)*.

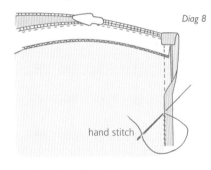

Diag 8

Repeat for the other side seam.

5. Shaping the base

At the base, separate the front from the back and finger press the marked fold lines on both sides of the purse. A point will form at the end of the folds. Pin and stitch across each end of the fold on the marked stitch lines *(diag 9)*.

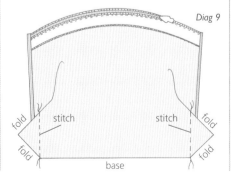

Diag 9

Trim away the point leaving a 6mm (1/4") seam allowance *(diag 10)*. Repeat at the opposite end.

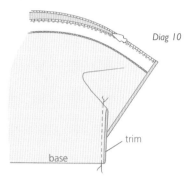

Diag 10

Cut two pieces of bias binding, each 8cm (3 1/8") long. Position the first fold of the binding on the stitch line ensuring that 1cm (3/8") of binding extends at each end. Bind the seams in the same manner as the side seams. Turn the purse to the right side and press.

6. Making the zip tab

Press under 6mm (1/4") on each long side of the tab and tack in place. Press under 6mm (1/4") on each end of the tab *(diag 11)*.

Diag 11

Take the tab through the large brass ring. Fold in half with wrong sides together and pin. Beginning at the ring, hand stitch the front to the back along one side, across the end and along the second side *(diag 12)*. Press.

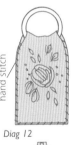

Diag 12

7. Finishing

Attach the large brass ring to the small brass ring. Attach the small brass ring to the zip pull tab *(diag 13)*.

Diag 13

Tissue holder

1. Preparation

Place the embroidered piece face down on a well padded surface, such as a folded flannelette sheet, and press. Cut out along the marked cutting lines.

2. Binding the opening edges

With right sides together, pin and stitch the lining to the damask across one short end. The lining is longer than the damask as it forms the binding on the front opening edges *(diag 1)*.

Diag 1

Repeat at the opposite end realigning the layers to ensure the raw edges are even. Trim the seam allowances to 5mm (3/16") and press towards the lining. Turn through to the right side. Press, ensuring 5mm (3/16") of lining shows as binding at each end of the damask *(diag 2)*.

Diag 2

With the damask facing up, 'stitch in the ditch' close to the binding through both layers of fabric *(diag 3)*.

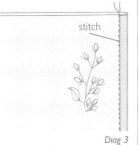

Diag 3

3. Forming the tissue holder

With lining sides together, fold the tissue holder so the bound edges meet at the centre *(diag 4)*.

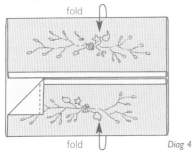

fold

fold

Diag 4

Press. Stitch across each side 1cm (3/8") from the raw edge. Press.

4. Binding the sides

With right sides together, place one moiré binding strip along one side of the tissue holder. Ensure the outer raw edges are even and the binding strip extends evenly beyond each side. Stitch along the previous stitch line *(diag 5)*.

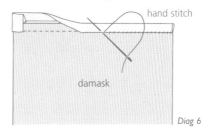

Diag 5

Trim the seam allowance to 5mm (3/16") and press the binding away from the tissue holder. Press under 5mm (3/16") on the remaining long raw edge of the binding. Turn under the ends and fold the binding over the seam allowance and to the back of the tissue holder. Hand stitch the folded edge of the binding to the previous stitch line *(diag 6)*.

hand stitch

damask

Diag 6

Bind the other side in the same manner.

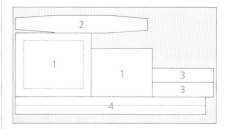

Blue Danube

For colour photos and full details, see pages 30 - 35.

CUTTING OUT

Where pattern pieces are not provided cut the pieces according to the measurements below.

Jacaranda silk dupion, fusible interfacing and shapewell

Cut one piece of each: 22cm x 28cm wide (8 5/8" x 11") for the front

Cut two pieces of each: 5cm x 22.5cm wide (2" x 8 7/8") for the top

Cut one piece each of jacaranda silk dupion and fusible interfacing: 70cm x 6cm wide (27 1/2" x 2 3/8") for the handle

Cut one piece of shapewell: 70cm x 4cm wide (27 1/2" x 1 1/2") for the handle

Ivory silk lining

Cut two pieces: 17cm x 22.5cm wide (6 3/4" x 8 7/8") for the front and back

CUTTING LAYOUTS

Jacaranda silk dupion, fusible interfacing and shapewell

1. Front and back
2. Base and sides
3. Top
4. Handle (Note the different width for the shapewell piece)

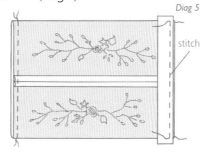

Ivory silk lining

2. Base and sides
5. Front and back

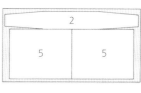

CONSTRUCTION

All seam allowances are 1cm (3/8") unless otherwise specified. The shaded areas on the following diagrams indicate the right side of the fabric.

1. Preparing the silk pieces

Fuse the interfacing to all pieces.

Mount all the fused silk pieces onto shapewell using long straight stitches, just inside the seam allowance. Centre the shapewell piece for the handle on the wrong side and baste in place along the length 5mm (3/16") in from each long edge. These stitches will be removed after construction.

Cut out the exact shape for the front once the embroidery is complete following the marked cutting lines.

2. Constructing the bag

With right sides together and matching raw edges, pin the front to the base and side piece. Stitch in between the notches, pivoting the needle at the corners. Clip into the corners of the base piece and at the notched points on the front *(diag 1)*.

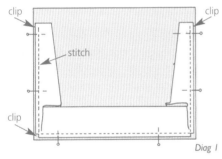

Diag 1

Pin and stitch the back piece to the base and sides in the same manner.

Press the side and base seams away from the front and back.

Place the piece of template plastic into the base of the bag so that it sits within the seam allowance. Using a doubled sewing thread, lace the plastic in position by stitching from side to side several times, through the seam allowance *(diag 2)*.

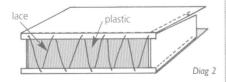

Diag 2

3. Attaching the zip

Pin and stitch each top piece to the zip *(diag 3)*.

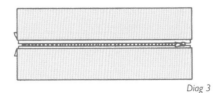

Diag 3

With right sides facing and matching raw edges, pin the prepared top in place along the back of the bag.

Stitch in place between the marked positions, pivoting the needle at the corners *(diag 4)*.

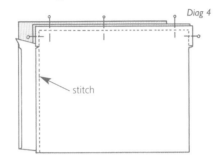

Diag 4

Trim the corners. Repeat for the front of the bag. Turn to the right side through the zip, carefully pushing out the top corners.

4. Constructing and attaching the handle

With right sides facing and matching raw edges pin and stitch the handle along the long edge.

Turn through to the right side and press so that the seam is centred along one side *(diag 5)*.

Diag 5

Pin each end of the handle to the top of each side matching raw edges and with the seam of the handle facing outwards. Stitch in place with two rows of stitching *(diag 6)*.

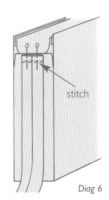

Diag 6

5. Constructing the lining

Following step 2 and omitting the plastic base, construct the lining in a similar manner to the bag, leaving a 10cm (4") opening on one long edge of the base *(diag 7)*.

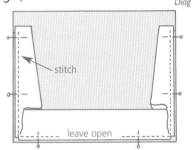

Diag 7

6. Attaching the lining

With right sides together, place the lining inside the bag. Matching raw edges, pin the lining to the top pieces, sandwiching the zip tapes between *(diag 8)*.

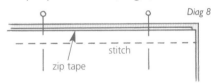

Diag 8

Turn through to the right side through the opening in the lining. Press the fabric and lining away from the zip.

7. Finishing

Handstitch the opening in the base of the lining closed.

At the inside of the handle and the ends of the top pieces, turn the seam allowances under and handstitch the lining to the bag *(diag 9)*.

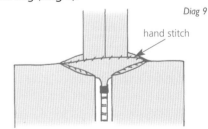

Diag 9

Topstitch along each side of the zip through all layers *(diag 10)*.

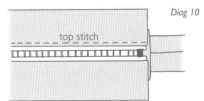

Diag 10

With the zip open, fold each top piece in half along the length so the lining lies flat. Catch the lining to the shapewell with very small stitches along the fold line *(diag 11)*.

Diag 11

Remove any basting stitches still showing. Bead the remaining section of the branch without catching the lining.

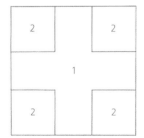

Summer Fruit

For colour photos and full details, see pages 36 - 47.

CUTTING OUT

Following the cutting layouts and referring to the instructions on page 38, cut out the bag and pockets from the damask and calico. Cut out all remaining embroidery requirements using the templates on this sheet.

CUTTING LAYOUTS

Ivory damask

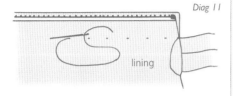

1. Bag
2. Pocket

Calico

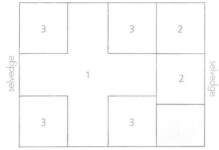

1. Bag lining
2. Pocket interlining
3. Internal pocket

Red homespun

4. Upper raspberry
5. Lower raspberry
6. Blackberry

Red felt

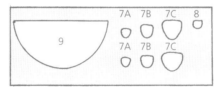

7. Strawberry padding (A, B and C)
8. Ladybird
9. Strawberry tassel

White felt   **Black felt**

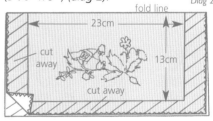

10. Strawberry flower   **11.** Blackberry tassel

Organza

12. Bee wings

Appliqué paper

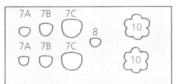

7. Strawberry padding (A, B and C)
8. Ladybird
10. Strawberry flower

CONSTRUCTION

*All seam allowances are 6mm (¹/₄")
unless otherwise specified. The shaded
areas on the following diagrams indicate
the right side of the fabric.*

1. Preparation

Trim away the calico from the unembroidered half of the pocket, cutting it back to the pressed fold line *(diag 1)*.

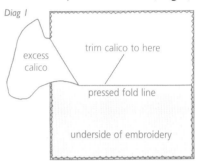

Diag 1

Place the embroidered fabric face down on a well padded surface, such as a folded flannelette sheet, and press.

With wrong sides together, fold all four pocket pieces in half and press.

Using the fold as the upper edge and ensuring the embroidery design is centred, cut along the three sides with the raw edges to obtain a folded rectangle measuring 13cm x 23cm wide (5 ¹/₈" x 9") *(diag 2)*.

Diag 2

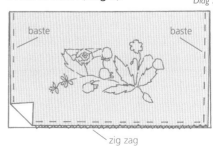

On each pocket, pin and baste the layers together along the sides and the lower edge. Neaten the lower edge of each pocket piece with a machine zigzag or overlock stitch *(diag 3)*.

Diag 3

2. Stay stitching the base

Beginning 4cm (1 5/8") away from one corner of the base, stitch along the stitch line until reaching the corner. Pivot and stitch along the second side for the same distance (diag 4).

Clip into the corner, taking care not to cut the stay stitching (diag 5).

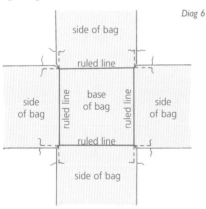

Repeat for the remaining corners. Using a vanishing fabric marker, rule lines between the corners of the stay stitching to indicate the stitch lines at the base of the bag (diag 6).

Diag 4 — side of bag / base of bag / side of bag

Diag 5 — clip / base of bag

Diag 6 — side of bag / ruled line / side of bag / base of bag / side of bag / ruled line / side of bag

3. Attaching the pockets

With right sides together and the embroidery design facing down, centre one pocket onto the base of the bag, aligning stitch lines. Pin in place.

Ensuring the seam allowances of the adjacent sides are out of the way and beginning and ending 6mm (1/4") from the sides of the pocket, stitch along the stitch line through the pocket and the base of the bag beneath (diag 7).

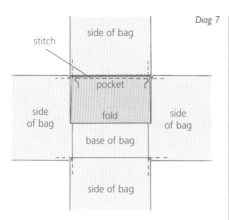

Diag 7 — stitch / side of bag / pocket / fold / side of bag / side of bag / base of bag / side of bag

Press the pocket away from the base. Tack the sides of the pocket to the sides of the bag. Repeat for the remaining three pockets ensuring the embroidery designs are placed on opposite sides of the bag (diag 8).

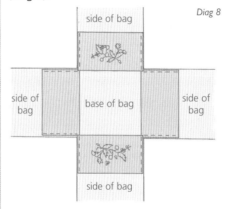

Diag 8 — side of bag / side of bag / base of bag / side of bag / side of bag

4. Stitching the sides

With right sides together and aligning the top of the pockets, pin two adjacent sides of the bag together. Beginning at the corner of the stay stitching and reinforcing the stitching at both ends, stitch along one side (diag 9).

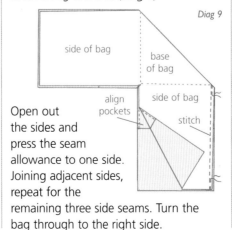

Diag 9 — side of bag / base of bag / align pockets / side of bag / stitch

Open out the sides and press the seam allowance to one side. Joining adjacent sides, repeat for the remaining three side seams. Turn the bag through to the right side.

5. Making the eyelets

Working on the damask, at one side seam measure down 4.5cm (1 3/4") from the top raw edge and stitch one eyelet 6mm (1/4") to the left of the seam. Repeat on the right of the seam (diag 10).

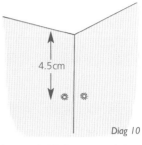

Diag 10 — 4.5cm

6. Making the lining

Recut the four internal pocket squares to each measure 26cm x 23cm wide (10 1/4" x 9"). Fold each lining pocket piece in half and press. Baste the raw edges together along three sides. Staystitch the corners of the lining base and attach the pockets in the same manner as the bag pockets.

Divide the internal pockets into storage sections by stitching a line through the centre of two pockets to divide them in half. Divide the remaining pockets into thirds and stitch in the same manner (diag 11).

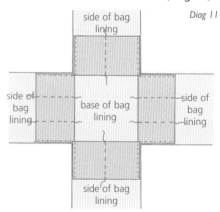

Diag 11 — side of bag lining / side of bag lining / base of bag lining / side of bag lining / side of bag lining

Complete the lining in the same manner as the damask bag.

7. Attaching the lining

Place the lining inside the bag with wrong sides together. Matching side seams, pin the two layers together around the top edge. Baste around the top of the bag approximately 3mm (1/8") in from the edge (diag 12).

Diag 12 — baste / baste

8. Attaching the ribbon binding

Press under 6mm (¼") at one raw end of the ribbon. With right sides together and placing the ribbon 6mm (¼") from the raw edge of the bag, pin the folded end of the ribbon to one side seam. Continue pinning the ribbon around the top edge of the bag, overlapping the folded end at the beginning. Trim any excess length of ribbon (diag 13).

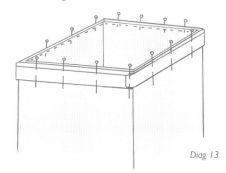

Diag 13

Stitch the ribbon to the bag using a 1cm (⅜") seam allowance on the damask. Press the ribbon away from the bag. Fold the remaining edge of the ribbon to the inside, aligning it with the previous stitch line. Pin and hand stitch in place (diag 14).

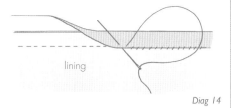

lining

Diag 14

9. Forming the casing

Using a vanishing fabric marker, rule a line around the entire bag, 4cm (1 ⅝") down from the top edge. Stitch along this line through both layers. Stitch another line 1cm (⅜") down from this line to form the casing. The eyelets should be centred between the two stitch lines (diag 15).

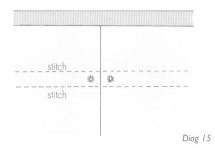

stitch

stitch

Diag 15

10. Making the twisted cord

Open out the whole 8m (8yd 27") skein of D. Fold in half and then in half again, forming a 2m (2yd 6 ¾") length. Place the strands together and make a twisted cord following the instructions on page 45. Repeat for the second skein of D.

Thread the cord through the entire casing and emerge in the eyelet adjacent to the start (diag 16).

Diag 16

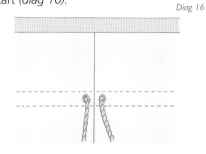

Whip the ends together. Starting and finishing on the opposite side of the bag, thread the second cord through the casing. Whip the ends together.

Attach the strawberry tassel to the end of one cord and the black-berry tassel to the remaining cord with tiny back stitches concealing the ends between the leaves (diag 17).

Diag 17

Fresh Fields

For colour photos and full details, see pages 48 - 53.

CUTTING OUT

Where pattern pieces are not provided cut the pieces according to the following measurements. The shaded areas on the following diagrams indicate the right side of the fabric.

Striped fabric

Bag: cut two, each 45cm x 43cm wide (17 ¾" x 17")

Handles: cut two, each 33cm x 8cm wide (13" x 3 ⅛"). Ensure these pieces are cut so that the stripes are evenly placed on the finished handles.

Interfacing

Embroidery backing: cut two, each 16cm x 26cm wide (6 ¾" x 10 ¼")

Top band: cut two, each 37cm x 7.5cm wide (14 ½" x 3") for the top band

Handles: cut two, each 33cm x 6cm wide (13" x 2 ⅜")

CUTTING LAYOUTS

Striped fabric

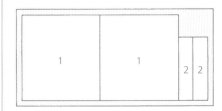

1. Front and Back
2. Handle

Interfacing

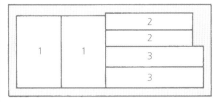

1. Embroidery backing
2. Handle
3. Top band

PREPARING THE EMBROIDERY

1. When the embroidery is complete, wash in cold water to remove any pencil marks. Pat with a clean towel. Place the embroidery face down on a well padded surface and press.

2. With wrong sides together, fold the fabric in half horizontally and press. Insert two pieces of interfacing. Turn under the raw edges along the previously tacked lines and pin (diag 1).

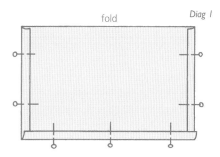

fold   *Diag 1*

3. Centre the embroidered panel over the striped bag front, 10cm (4'') down from the top raw edge.

4. Pin and attach the embroidered piece with small hand stitches. Remove the tacking.

CONSTRUCTION

For step - by - step instructions for making the bag, see pages 52 - 53.

Celadon

For colour photos and full details, see pages 54 - 57.

CUTTING OUT

Where pattern pieces are not provided cut the pieces according to the measurements below.

Willow green shot silk dupion

Cut one piece 6.5cm x 18cm wide (2 1/2" x 7") for the base

Cut two pieces, each 4.5cm x 31cm wide (1 3/4" x 12 1/4") for the handles

Woven fusible interfacing, shapewell and lining

Cut one piece of each 6.5cm x 18cm wide (2 1/2" x 7") for the base

CUTTING LAYOUTS

Willow green shot silk dupion

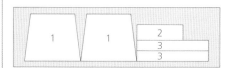

1. Front and back **2.** Base **3.** Handles

Woven fusible interfacing, shapewell and lining
1. Front and back
2. Base

CONSTRUCTION

All seam allowances are 1cm (3/8") unless otherwise specified. The shaded areas on the following diagrams indicate the right side of the fabric.

1. Preparing the silk for embroidery and beading

Fuse the interfacing to the silk front, back and base pieces. Place the shapewell onto the back of the silk pieces and baste in place along all edges using a long machine stitch. Overlock or machine zigzag along all raw edges of the front piece. Complete the embroidery following the instructions on pages 55 - 57.

2. Constructing the bag

With right sides together and matching centre points, pin the base to the back piece and stitch (*diag 1*).

Diag 1

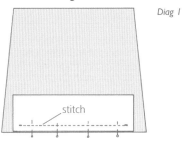

stitch

With right sides together, pin and stitch the remaining long side of the base to the front piece. Press the seams towards the base. With right sides together and matching raw edges, pin the front to the back at the sides and stitch. Press the seams open. Position one side seam onto the base. Pin and stitch, clipping the corners on the bag piece (*diag 2*).

Repeat for the remaining side of the bag. Place the template plastic onto the base of the bag, so it sits underneath the seam allowance. Using a double

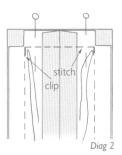

stitch
clip
Diag 2

sewing thread, lace the plastic in position by stitching from side to side several times, through the seam allowance (*diag 3*).

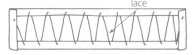

lace

Diag 3

Turn the bag to the right side.

3. Handles

With right sides together, fold the pieces of silk for the handles in half along the length and stitch.

Turn each piece through to the right side. Thread a length of piping cord through each piece.
Position each end of one handle 2.5cm (1") from each side seam.
Stitch each end securely in place onto the seam allowance (*diag 4*). Repeat with the second handle on the remaining side.

2.5cm   stitch

Diag 4

4. Constructing the lining

Make the lining in the same manner as the bag, leaving a 13cm (5") opening on one long side of the base (*diag 5*).

Diag 5

leave open

5. Attaching the lining

With right sides together, place the lining over the bag. Pin and stitch around the top (*diag 6*).

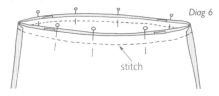

Diag 6

stitch

Press the seams towards the lining. Turn the lining to the right side through the opening in the base.

6. Finishing

Handstitch the opening in the base of the lining closed.

Push the lining into the bag and press gently with a warm iron.

Home Coming

For colour photos and full details, see pages 58 - 61.

CUTTING OUT

Where pattern pieces are not provided, cut the pieces according to the measure-ments below.

Black wool cashmere velour

Rectangle for bag: cut one, 44cm x 16cm wide (17 $^3/_8$" x 6 $^3/_8$")

Handle: cut two, each 26cm x 6cm wide (10 $^1/_4$" x 2 $^3/_8$")

Red wool cashmere velour

Strips for roses: tear two, 150cm x 6cm wide (59" x 2 $^3/_8$")

Red satin

Bag lining: cut one, 44cm x 16cm wide (17 $^3/_8$" x 6 $^3/_8$")

Interfacing

Handle: cut two, each 26cm x 6cm wide (10 $^1/_4$" x 2 $^3/_8$")

CUTTING LAYOUTS

Black wool cashmere velour

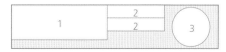

1. Bag **2.** Handles **3.** Base

Red satin

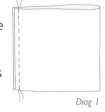

1. Lining
2. Base

CONSTRUCTION

1. Side seam

Fuse interfacing to the wrong side of the wool cashmere bag piece. With right sides together and matching raw edges, pin and stitch the bag along the side seam *(diag 1)*. Press the seam open.

Diag 1

2. Attaching the base

Pin and baste the buckram to the wrong side of the wool cashmere base. With right sides together and matching marks, pin and stitch the bag to the base *(diag 2)*.

Diag 2

Trim and neaten the seam. Turn to the right side and top stitch 4mm ($^3/_{16}$") from the seam around the entire base.

3. Assembling the lining

Pin and stitch the lining side seam in the same manner as the bag, leaving a 5cm (2") opening for turning *(diag 3)*.

Diag 3

With right sides together and matching marks, pin and stitch the base lining to the bag lining. With right sides together and matching side seams, pin the bag to the lining around the top edge. Stitch *(diag 4)*.

Diag 4

Trim and neaten the seam. Turn to the right side and press gently. Topstitch 3mm ($^1/_8$") from the upper edge around the bag. Topstitch a further 2 rows, each spaced 3mm ($^1/_8$") apart.

4. Making the handles

Fuse the interfacing to the wrong side of each handle strip. With right sides together and matching raw edges, pin and stitch each strip along the long raw edges using a 6mm ($^1/_2$") seam allowance *(diag 5)*.

Diag 5

Turn to the right side and press. Neaten the raw ends of each handle. Pin each handle to the top of the bag spacing them 5cm (2") apart as shown in the diagram. Stitch two rows along the previous topstitched rows to secure *(diag 6)*.

Diag 6

5. Attaching the roses

Make nine large folded roses and four leaves following the step-by-step instructions on pages 60 and 61.

Attach one leaf to the centre of the bag approximately 2cm ($^3/_4$") from the base, with matching machine sewing thread and small hand stitches to the wool cashmere layer only *(diag 7)*.

Diag 7

Attach the remaining three leaves on the other side of the bag in the same manner as shown *(diag 8)*.

Handstitch the roses around the lower edge of the bag, forming a circle.

Diag 8

All Roses

For colour photos and full details, see pages 62 - 65.

CUTTING OUT

Where pattern pieces are not provided cut the pieces according to the measurements on the following page.

Furnishing fabric

Cut one 35cm (14") square for the front of the bag.

Fusible wadding

Cut one 35cm (14") square for the front of the bag.

CUTTING LAYOUTS

Furnishing fabric

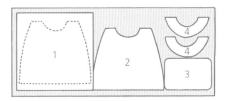

1. Front   **3.** Base
2. Back   **4.** Facing

Calico

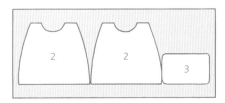

2. Front and back   **3.** Base

Fusible wadding

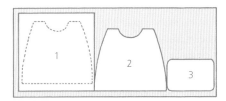

1. Front   **3.** Base
2. Back

CONSTRUCTION

All seam allowances are 1cm (³/8") unless otherwise specified. The shaded areas on the following diagrams indicate the right side of the fabric.

1. Attaching the wadding

Place the embroidery face down on a well padded surface and fuse the wadding in place, pressing gently so that the embroidery is not flattened.

Cut out the shape of the front following the marked cutting lines. Fuse the wadding to the wrong side of the back and base.

2. Constructing the bag

With right sides together and matching raw edges, pin the front to the back at the sides. Stitch the sides to the marked position *(diag 1)*.

Diag 1

Press the seams open, including the unstitched section of the sides. With right sides together, pin the base to the bag. Tack and stitch, easing the fabric around the corners to avoid puckering *(diag 2)*.

Diag 2

Fold under the seam allowance at each end of one facing piece and press. With right sides together and matching raw edges, place the facing over the back of the bag. Pin and stitch *(diag 3)*.
Attach the remaining facing to the front in the same manner.

Diag 3

3. Constructing the lining

Make the lining in the same manner as the bag, leaving a 13cm (5") opening on one long edge of the base *(diag 4)*.

Diag 4

4. Attaching the lining

With right sides together, place the lining inside the bag. Pin and stitch across the top without catching the facing ends *(diag 5)*.

Clip around the curved edge and trim.

Diag 5

Pin one section of a side opening and stitch to the previous stitching at the marked point, keeping the other section out of the way *(diag 6)*.

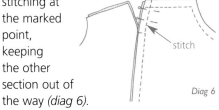
Diag 6

Pin and stitch the second half of the opening. Repeat for the remaining side opening. Place the plastic base into the base of the bag so that it sits within the seam allowance *(diag 7)*.

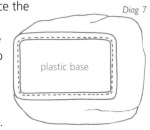
Diag 7

Using a double sewing thread, lace the plastic in position by stitching from side to side several times, through the seam allowance *(diag 8)*.

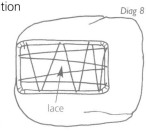
Diag 8

Turn to the right side through the opening in the lining base. Press the facings towards the lining.

5. Inserting the handles

Place one handle between the lining and the facing and tack in place. Turn under the seam allowance of the facing and hand stitch in place *(diag 9)*.

Diag 9

Using a zipper foot, stitch as close as possible to the handle through all layers *(diag 10)*.

Repeat for the remaining handle.

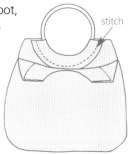

stitch

Diag 10

6. Finishing

Handstitch the opening in the base of the lining closed.

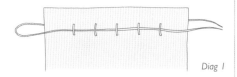

Vintage

For colour photos and full details, see pages 66 - 75.

CONSTRUCTION

All seam allowances are 2cm (³/4") unless otherwise specified. The shaded areas on the following diagrams indicate the right side of the fabric.

1. Making the twisted cord

Make two cords following the instructions on page 45. For each one, cut a 3m (3yds 10") length of A. Fold in half and knot the loose ends together.

2. Inserting the twisted cord

Thread one cord through the loops from the right hand side, around the bag and back to the starting point *(diag 1)*.

Diag 1

Tie the ends of the cord together with a thread. Repeat with the remaining cord, starting from the left hand side of the bag.

3. Make the tassels following these step-by-step instructions.

For each tassel, cut a 6m (6yd 20") length of C.

1. 2.

1. Fold in half five times until the bundle of thread is approximately 18cm (7") in length. Tie in the middle.

2. Loop the threads over the tied end of the twisted cord, ensuring it is centred. Tie the tassel firmly to keep in place on the cord.

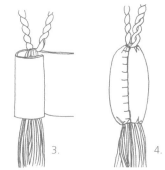

3. 4.

3. Forming the head. Cut a piece of felt 10cm x 2.5cm wide (4" x 1") and wrap around the tassel head.

4. Stitch in place, drawing in the top and base to give a rounded shape.

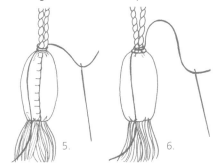

5. 6.

5. Using the tapestry needle and leaving a tail the length of the skirt, wrap three strands of A twice around the cord as close as possible to the tassel.

6. Work a row of detached blanket stitch into the wrapped threads.

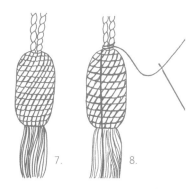

7. 8.

7. Continue working detached blanket stitch until the felt is covered.

8. Bars. Wrap three strands of B twice around the cord where it joins the tassel head, again leaving a tail the length of the skirt.

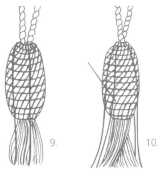

9. 10.

9. Work detached blanket stitch into the wraps. Leave threads hanging the length of the skirt to form the first bar foundation.

10. For the second bar, thread three strands of B through the blanket stitch band so that there are two lengths from top to bottom.

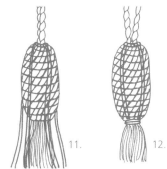

11. 12.

11. Repeat for the remaining two bar foundations, ensuring that all four are evenly spaced.

12. Hold the four pairs of thread in place and wrap firmly with three strands of A at the base of the tassel head.

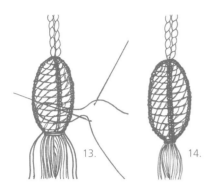

13. 14.

13. Work double detached blanket stitch down each bar in the same manner as the cord loops. Maintain tension by pulling the ends down as necessary.

14. Wrap twice around the base of the head, leaving a tail as before.

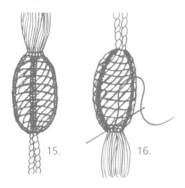

15. 16.

15. Turn the tassel upside down and work detached blanket stitch around the wraps. Leave the working thread and tail to form part of the skirt.

16. With one strand of thread in the milliner's needle, couch the ring to the base of the head.

4. Lining the bag

With right sides together, join the side seams of the lining fabric. Turn the upper edge under 2cm (³/₄") and tack. Press the lining and place inside the bag (*diag 2*).

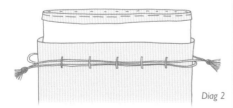

Diag 2

Hand stitch the lining in place 1cm (³/₈") below the upper edge of the bag (*diag 3*).

Diag 3

5. Finishing

Remove all tacking stitches. Cut, trim and comb the tassel ends.

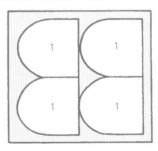

Cherish

For colour photos and full details, see pages 76 - 79.

CUTTING OUT

Cut out all pieces according to the cutting layout.

CUTTING LAYOUT

Cream cotton voile

1. Front, back and lining

CONSTRUCTION

All seam allowances are 1cm (³/₈") unless otherwise specified. The shaded areas on the following diagrams indicate the right side of the fabric.

1. Preparation

When the embroidery is complete, place the fabric face down on a well padded surface and press.

2. Joining the front to the back

Place the front and back together with right sides facing. Pin and baste the sides

and lower edge of the bag. Stitch (*diag 1*). Trim the seam allowance to 6mm (¹/₄"). Turn to the right side and press.

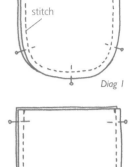

Diag 1

3. Making the lining

Stitch the two lining pieces together in the same manner as the bag, leaving an opening of 5cm (2") on the lower edge (*diag 2*). Trim the seam allowance to 6mm (¹/₄") and press.

Diag 2

4. Attaching the lining

With right sides together, slip the lining over the bag. Pin and baste the bag and lining together around the top edges (*diag 3*). Stitch.

Diag 3

Turn the bag to the right side through the opening in the lining. Slip stitch the opening closed (*diag 4*). Push the lining into the bag and press.

5. Attaching the lace edging and lace beading

Roll a narrow hem on each end of the narrow lace edging and hand stitch. Pull the gimp thread in the lace heading so the gathered lace fits evenly around the sides and lower edge of the bag.

Pin one end of the lace 15mm (⁵/₈") from the top of the bag on one side seam (*diag 5*).

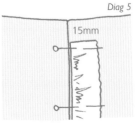

Diag 4

Diag 5

Continue pinning the lace along the seam, until 15mm ($^5/8$") from the upper edge on the other side (*diag 6*). Hand stitch the lace in place using tiny stitches.

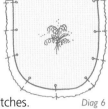

Diag 6

Starting and finishing at the centre back, attach the wider lace edging to the upper edge of the bag in the same manner. Whip the raw ends together to finish (*diag 7*).

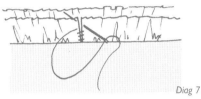

Diag 7

Starting at the centre front, pin the lace beading around the upper edge of the bag, just below the lace edging. When returning to the centre front, overlap the ends and trim away any excess lace beading (*diag 8*).

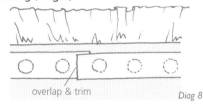

overlap & trim

Diag 8

In order to centre the bow you will need an even number of holes.

Attach both edges of the beading using tiny slip stitches, ensuring the stitches go through both the bag and the lining.

6. Finishing

Starting at the centre front, thread the ribbon through the beading. Tie into a bow and trim the tails diagonally.

Gidget

For colour photos and full details, see pages 80 - 83.

CUTTING OUT

Where pattern pieces are not provided, cut the pieces according to the measurements below.

Pink cotton poplin

Bag: cut one, 20cm x 28cm wide (8" x 11")

Handle: cut two, each 5cm x 26cm wide (2" x 10$^1/4$")

Lime cotton gingham

Frill: cut one, 4cm x 90cm wide (1$^5/8$" x 35$^1/2$")

Lining: cut one, 20cm x 28cm wide (8" x 11")

CUTTING LAYOUTS

Pink cotton poplin

1. Bag
2. Handle
3. Heart

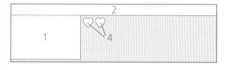

Lime cotton gingham

1. Lining **2.** Handle **4.** Heart

CONSTRUCTION

See page 82.

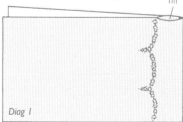

Perfumed Memories

For colour photos and full details, see pages 84 - 87.

CUTTING OUT

Where pattern pieces are not provided cut the pieces according to the measurements below.

Silk dupion

Bag: cut 2, each 64.5cm x 37.5cm wide (25$^1/2$" x 14$^3/4$")

Sash: cut one, 121cm x 23cm wide (47$^1/2$" x 9")

Silk organza

Pocket: cut one, 14cm x 37.5cm wide (5$^1/2$" x 14$^3/4$") for the pocket

CUTTING LAYOUT

Silk dupion

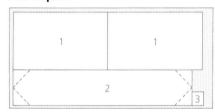

1. Front and Back **2.** Tie **3.** Tab

CONSTRUCTION

All seam allowances are 1cm ($^3/8$") unless otherwise specified. The shaded areas on the following diagrams indicate the right side of the fabric.

1. Preparation

When the embroidery is complete, place the fabric face down on a well-padded surface and press carefully.

2. Assembling the bag

With right sides together, pin the front to the back at the sides and lower edge. Stitch down one side and across the lower edge. Turn to the right side and fill the organza pocket with lavender (*diag 1*).

fill

Diag 1

Turn to the wrong side and stitch the remaining side seam (*diag 2*). Neaten all edges.

stitch

Diag 2

Turn the upper edge down 1cm (³/8") to the inside and then a further 10cm (4"). Hand stitch the hem *(diag 3)*.

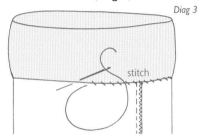

Diag 3

Turn the bag to the right side and carefully push out the corners.

3. Making the sash

With right sides together fold the sash piece in half along the length. Starting at the folded edge, stitch across one end at a 45 degree angle towards the open edge. Pivot and stitch down the long side. Repeat at the remaining end leaving a small section open *(diag 4)*.

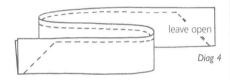

Diag 4

Trim the ends, turn to the right side and hand stitch the opening closed.

4. Making the tab

Fold in half across the length and with right sides together, stitch the long edge. Press the seam open. Turn the tab to the right side so that the seam is at the centre back. Turn the raw ends in 1cm (³/8") and hand stitch *(diag 5)*.

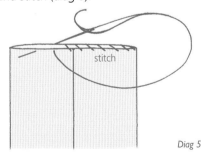

Diag 5

With the embroidery facing out, centre the tab 1cm (³/8") below the hem stitch line on the back. Attach the upper edge of the tab with small hand stitches. Measure down 5cm (2") and attach the lower edge at this position *(diag 6)*.

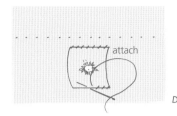

Diag 6

Thread the sash through the tab and tie in a bow around the front of the bag.

Midnight Fantasy

For colour photos and full details, see pages 88 - 91.

CUTTING OUT

Trace pattern piece G (on the liftout sheet) onto lightweight interfacing or tracing paper, transferring the pattern markings. Where pattern pieces are not provided, cut the pieces according to the measurements below. Cut out all the pieces following the cutting layouts.

Fuchsia satin-backed shantung

Front band: cut one, 8cm x 122cm wide (3 ¼" x 48")

Front and back lining: cut two, 33.6cm x 31.5cm wide (13 ¼" x 12 ³/8")

Pocket: cut two, 12cm x 19cm wide (4 ³/4" x 7 ¹/2")

Black quilted satin

Front side panels: cut two, 28cm x 14.2cm wide (11" x 5 ⁵/8")

Back: cut one, 28cm x 31.5cm wide (11" x 12 ³/8")

Top panels: cut two, 6.5cm x 31.5cm wide (2 ¹/2" x 12 ³/8")

Handles: cut two, 8cm x 59cm wide (3" x 23 ¹/4")

Interfacing

Front side panels: cut two, as for black quilted satin

Back: cut one, as for black quilted satin

Top panels: cut two, as for black quilted satin

Handles: cut two, 4cm x 59cm wide (1 ¹/2" x 23 ¹/4")

CUTTING LAYOUTS

Fuchsia satin-backed shantung

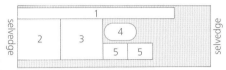

Fuchsia satin-back shantung, 150cm (59") wide

1. Front band   **2.** Front lining
3. Back lining   **4.** Base (G)   **5.** Pocket

Black quilted satin

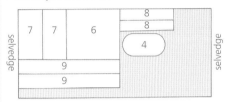

Black quilted satin, 112cm (44") wide

4. Base (G)   **6.** Back   **7.** Front side panel
8. Top panel   **9.** Handle

Interfacing

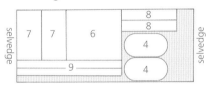

Interfacing, 112cm (44") wide

4. Base (G)   **6.** Back   **7.** Front side panel
8. Top panel   **9.** Handle

Template Plastic

4. Base (G)

CONSTRUCTION

All seam allowances are 1cm (³/8") unless otherwise specified. The shaded areas on the following diagrams indicate the right side of the fabric.

1. Making the lining pocket

With right sides together and matching raw edges, pin the two pocket pieces together. Stitch around the outside, leaving 7.5cm (3") for turning *(diag 1)*.

Diag 1

Clip the corners, turn to the right side and press. Topstitch 1cm (³/8") from the upper edge of the pocket *(diag 2)*.

Diag 2

2. Attaching the pocket to the back lining

Centre the pocket on the right side of the back lining, aligning the top of the pocket 7cm (2³/4") from the top raw edge. Pin and stitch around the sides and lower edge *(diag 3)*.

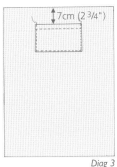

7cm (2³/4")

Diag 3

3. Lining side seams

With right sides together and matching raw edges, pin and stitch the bag front and back lining pieces together at the sides. Trim and neaten the seams *(diag 4)*. Press.

Diag 4

4. Attaching the lining base

Fuse the interfacing to the wrong side of the base lining. Attach the base to the lining in the same manner as the quilted bag, leaving a 15cm (6") opening for turning.

5. Making the handles

Fuse interfacing to the wrong side of the upper half of each handle piece *(diag 5)*.

fold

Diag 5

On each long side of one handle piece, fold under 1cm (³/8") and press. With wrong sides together, fold the handle in half along the length and press. Pin the folded edges together *(diag 6)*.

Diag 6

Stitch approximately 2mm (¹/16") from the edge.

Topstitch the same distance from the other folded edge. Repeat for the remaining handle.

6. Attaching the handles

Turn the bag to the right side. On the top edge of the bag front, measure 5.5cm (2³/8") from each side seam and mark. Repeat for the bag back. Aligning the outer edge of the handle with the marks, pin and baste to the inside front of the bag *(diag 7)*.

Diag 7

Repeat for the remaining handle on the back.

7. Attaching the bag lining

With right sides together and matching raw edges and side seams, pin the lining to the bag around the upper edge. Stitch, back stitching at the handles to reinforce *(diag 8)*.

Turn the lining to the right side. Hand stitch the lining closed *(diag 9)*.

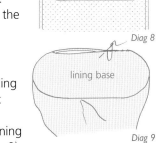

lining

Diag 8

lining base

Diag 9

8. Finishing

Stitch a row of tacking 1cm (³/8") from the upper edge of the bag *(diag 10)*.

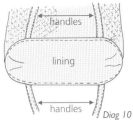

handles

lining

handles

Diag 10

Cut a piece of green frilled ribbon to fit around the outer edge of the bag allowing 1cm (³/8") extending at each end. Using the tacking as a guide for placement, pin and stitch in the same manner, with the ruffle towards the top of the bag.

Using the chalk fabric marker, measure and mark a line half way between the green ribbons on the top panel *(diag 11)*.

chalk line

Diag 11

Cut a length of braid to fit around the top of the bag plus 1cm (³/8"). Fold under 5mm (³/16") at each end and pin in place, beginning at a side seam as before. Hand stitch ensuring the stitches do not go through the lining.

Cut three pieces of braid to fit between the piped edges of the smocked band. Fold under the raw ends of one piece of braid and attach to the band 9.5cm (3³/4") from the top edge, taking care not to catch the lining.

Attach the second and third pieces 6cm (2³/8") apart in the same manner *(diag 12)*.

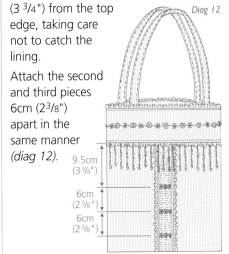

Diag 12

9.5cm (3³/4")

6cm (2³/8")

6cm (2³/8")

Bird of Paradise

For colour photos and full details, see pages 92 - 97.

CUTTING OUT

Cut a 41cm x 30.5cm wide (16" x 12") rectangle for the flap and back of the bag. This will be cut to its exact shape after the embroidery is complete.

Trace the pattern pieces onto lightweight interfacing or tracing paper.

Cut out all pieces following the cutting layouts and transfer the pattern markings.

CUTTING LAYOUTS

Black linen

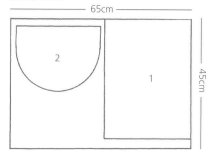

1. Back and flap
2. Front

Black polyester lining

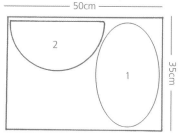

1. Back and flap lining
2. Front lining

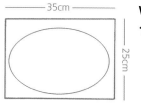

Wadding

1. Back and flap

CONSTRUCTION

All seam allowances are 1cm (³/8") unless otherwise specified.

1. Preparation

Place the embroidered section face down on a well padded surface. Cover with a cloth and press. Cut out the embroidered back and flap to the exact shape. Fuse the wadding to the wrong side of the embroidered piece.

2. Forming the darts

With right sides together, fold the dart in the front of the bag. Pin and stitch. Press the dart to one side *(diag 1).*

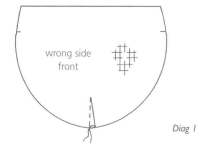

Diag 1

Repeat for the front lining.

3. Joining the front lining

With right sides together, pin the front lining to the bag front along the straight edge. Stitch, leaving an 8cm (3 ") opening in the centre *(diag 2)*. Open the pieces out and press the seam towards the lining.

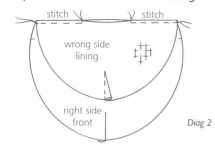

Diag 2

4. Attaching the elastic

With the wrong side facing you, position the elastic on the bag front just below the foldline indicated on the pattern. Pin and baste the ends *(diag 3)*.

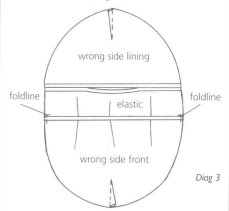

Diag 3

5. Attaching the back

With right sides together, matching edges and keeping the lining out of the way, pin the bag front to the back below the marked foldline. Stitch. Double stitch the elastic to secure. Stitch again 6mm (¹/4") away within the seam allowance *(diag 4)*. Trim the seam close to the second line of stitching and press.

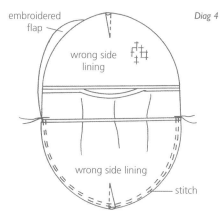

Diag 4

6. Attaching the lining

With right sides together and matching raw edges, pin the flap lining to the flap between the marks indicated at the foldline on the pattern. Stitch, beginning and ending at the marks. Stitch again 6mm (¹/4") away within the seam allowance *(diag 5)*. Trim the seam close to the second line of stitching and press.

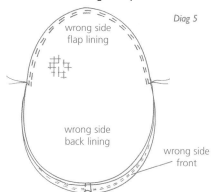

Diag 5

With right sides together and matching raw edges, pin the front lining to the back lining. Stitch, beginning and ending at the marked foldline. Stitch again 6mm (¹/4") away within the seam allowance *(diag 6)*. Trim the seam close to the second line of stitching and press.

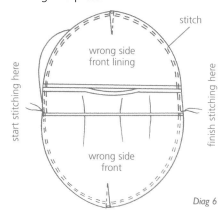

Diag 6

7. Forming the elastic casing

Turn the bag to the right side through the opening. Hold the elastic along the fold-line while pushing the lining to the inside.

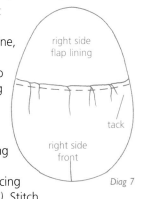

With the elastic positioned just below the foldline, fold the top of the bag front to the inside along the foldline to form a 4cm (1 1/2") deep facing. Stretching the elastic, pin and tack the facing in place *(diag 7)*. Stitch 1.5cm (5/8") from the fold to form the elastic casing. Slipstitch the opening closed.

right side flap lining

tack

right side front

Diag 7

8. Attaching the cord

Tie a knot in each end of the rayon cord. Position one knot inside the bag, 1cm (3/8") below the top of the casing at one side seam. Secure with several back stitches *(diag 8)*. Attach the remaining knot to the other side of the bag in the same manner.

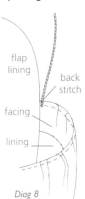

flap lining

back stitch

facing

lining

Diag 8

9. Finishing

Attach the Chinese ball button to the centre of the flap on the seam. Attach the top of the tassel head to the front of the bag at the mark indicated on the pattern.

Bonnie Wee Bag

For colour photos and full details, see pages 98 - 103.

CONSTRUCTION

All seam allowances are 1cm (3/8") unless otherwise specified. The shaded areas on the following diagrams indicate the right side of the fabric.

1. Assembling the bag

Undo approximately 3cm (1 1/4") of the tacking at each end of the upper edge. With right sides together, join the sides of the bag. With one strand of the stone thread (D), hand stitch the hem. Ensure that the stitches are not visible on the front of the bag.

2. Making the twisted cord

Make two cords following the instructions on page 45. For each one, cut a 2.9m (3yds 6") length of F. Fold in half and knot the loose ends together.

3. Inserting the twisted cord

Thread one cord through the loops from the right hand side, around the bag and back to the starting point *(diag 1)*.

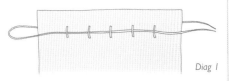

Diag 1

Tie the ends of the cord together. Repeat with the remaining cord, starting from the left hand side of the bag.

4. Making the tassels

Cut two 1.5m (1yd 24") lengths each of A, B and C. Fold in half four times, as for the thistle head, and tie in the centre *(diag 2)*. Loop the bunch of threads over the knotted end of the twisted cord *(diag 3)*. Ensure that it is centred. Tie the tassel firmly with two strands of the green thread approximately 2cm (3/4") from the cord *(diag 4)*. Thread the tapestry needle with three strands of the green thread. Holding the thread against the tassel

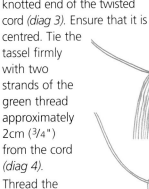

tie

Diag 2

Diag 3

Diag 4

tie

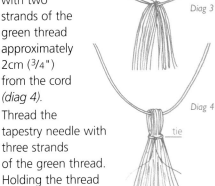

with your thumb, approximately 5cm (2") from the end, wrap the thread twice around the tassel *(diag 5)*.

Diag 5

wrap

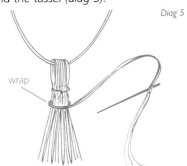

Work detached blanket stitch on the wrapped thread, incorporating the tail in the first two or three stitches. The remainder of the tail will be covered by the detached blanket stitch. Continue working until the cord is reached and secure the thread.

Trim the tassel ends and tail of green thread if necessary.

5. Lining the bag

With right sides together, join the side seams of the lining fabric. Turn the upper edge under 1cm (3/8") and tack. Press the lining and place inside the bag *(diag 6)*.

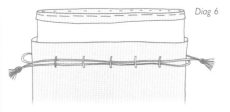

Diag 6

Hand stitch the lining in place 5mm (3/16") below the upper edge of the bag *(diag 7)*.

stitch

Diag 7

6. Finishing

Remove all tacking stitches.
Comb the tassel ends.

Back Stitch

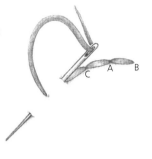

Blanket Stitch

1

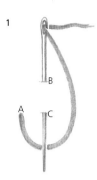

2

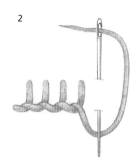

Buttonhole Stitch

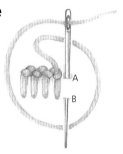

Bullion Knot

1

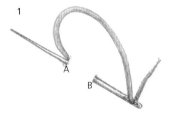

Bring thread to front at A. Pick up fabric the required length of the finished knot.

2

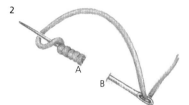

Wind enough wraps around needle to cover required distance.

3

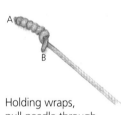

Holding wraps, pull needle through.

4

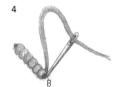

Insert needle at B.

5

Bullion Loop

A loop is formed when A and B are very close and many wraps are used.

Chain Stitch

1

2

3

Coral Stitch

Colonial Knot

1

2

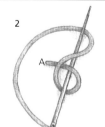

3

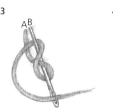

4

Couching

Laid thread is attached using a second thread.

Detached Blanket Stitch

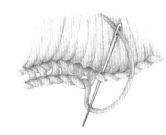

Work the detached stitches into some or all of the loops formed by previously worked blanket stitch.

Detached Chain

1 **2** **3**

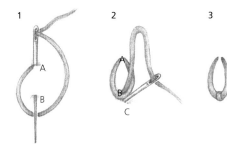

French Knot

1 **2** **3**

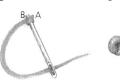

Grab Stitch

1 **2** **3**

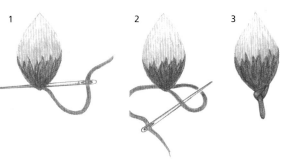

Padded Satin Stitch

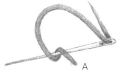

1 - *Satin Stitch*   **2** - *Split Stitch*   **3** - *Seed Stitch*

A variety of stitches can be used for the padding, which is then covered with satin stitch.

Running Stitch

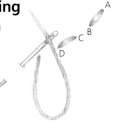

Satin Stitch

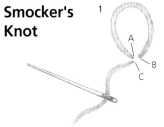

Smocker's Knot

1 **2**

3 **4** **5**

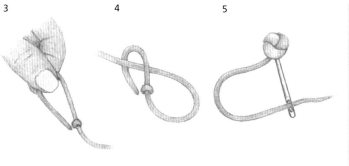

Split Back Stitch

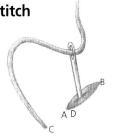

Stem Stitch

The thread is always kept below the needle.

Susan O'Connor

Susan maintains a busy teaching programme in Australia and the US.

Her background in fine arts and drawing and her love of textiles and threads are obvious in all her work, from heirloom garments to raised Elizabethan stumpwork. A regular contributor to publications for Country Bumpkin, where she is also editor-at-large, Susan is known for the perfection she achieves in design and workmanship.

Kris Richards

Always an enthusiastic seamstress, Kris discovered embroidery about ten years ago and now loves to combine her two passions. Her inspiration comes from old-fashioned gift cards and wrapping, wallpapers and china, and of course her garden. She has embroidered hundreds of beautiful bullion roses and still finds new ways of incorporating them into her designs. While soft wools and voiles are her favourites, she also appreciates the effect of more robust fabrics, such as natural linen, as a foil for her work.

Angela Watson

Angela has always been interested in textiles and this evolved into a passion for dressmaking, patchwork and quilting as well as embroidery.

As a teacher of embroidery, she enjoys creating designs which are not only pretty, but also practical, for her students.

Anna Scott

Born in Denmark, Anna trained at the Danish Needlecraft Guild College. Here she gained practical skills in a wide range of embroidery techniques as well as art history, design and adult education. In Australia, she teaches and works as an editor for Country Bumpkin and *Inspirations* magazine, to which she also contributes projects.

Her favourite techniques are crewelwork, for its endless choice of stitches, metal thread work and bead embroidery.

Jan Kerton

Jan was taught to sew by her grandmothers and the love of textile crafts has continued throughout her life. Her business Windflower Smocking specialises in the design and mail order of a delightful range of embroidered wool blankets using her unique appliqué technique. Jan also contributes regularly to Inspirations magazine and teaches a wide range of embroidery techniques locally, interstate and overseas.

Joan Gibson

Joan lives and teaches in Sydney. As a child she loved to make dolls clothes and her love of embroidery has developed from this passion. Her main inspiration comes from her cottage garden and is reflected in the themes of her projects. The field and hedgerow flowers of England have also influenced her designs.

Judy Stephenson

Judy has been exhibiting and successfully entering competitions since 1995. She lives in Queensland where she occasionally teaches workshops. She has a special talent for interpreting plants and flowers in raised embroidery, often set on a casalguidi-style background. Several of her original pieces have been published.

Alla Akselrod

A graduate of the Moscow Academy of Fine Arts, Alla now lives in Melbourne where she produces exquisite hand embroidered heirloom items. She has also created a range of delightful and enormously popular white stuffed animals, all elaborately embroidered in threads and ribbon, for *Inspirations* magazine.

Julie Graue

A perfectionist in everything, Julie is famous for her exquisitely smocked and embroidered children's garments. While pretty pastels are her trademark, she also has an eye for combining bright colours, especially pinks and greens, in stunning projects. Julie teaches regularly, encouraging her students to become accomplished and passionate needle-workers.

Jenny Crowe

Jenny is an artist in both watercolour and thread, sometimes combining the two in evocative tableaux. She holds regular exhibitions of her work and teaches embroidery to a loyal following. Although she has illustrated several books on historical buildings, her themes are generally inspired by her garden.